COUNTRY COMMUNE COOKING

COUNTRY COMMUNE

COOKING

by Lucy Horton

Illustrated by Judith St. Soleil

COWARD, McCANN & GEOGHEGAN, INC.
New York

To all commune people everywhere

Acknowledgment

My first and deepest thanks of course go to the people who contributed the recipes in this book, but to name them would reveal their carefully disguised identities. Thank you, good people. You've blown my mind. Love and thanks are also due to my true friends Mary and Robert Houriet of far Vermont; hospitable Californians Dr. William and Connie Price, Christine Joy, Jack Travis and Sue Thiemann; Mrs. J. Horton Ljams and my parents, Carolyn and Donald Horton, of New York City; Walter Lucas of Scottsdale, Arizona; Orle Ellison of Denver, friend to hitchhikers, and his gracious mother; and discriminating tasters Albert Driver, Richard Lorber, Neil Smith and Steve Crevoshay.
It's been grand, folks.

SBN: 698-10456-0

Library of Congress Catalog Card Number: 72-76673

Printed in the United States of America

Contents

III. MEAT (AND ONE FISH)   81

COUNTRY COMMUNE
COOKING

Introduction

When I arrived in San Francisco in June, 1971, I looked up my streetwise friend Jack, who always has an angle. "I'm writing a commune cookbook," I told him. "I'm going to visit country communes and collect their recipes."

"That's a great idea," Jack agreed enthusiastically. "Out in the country, food is what's happening."

The idea for this book had come from a similar remark. The winter before I had lived in northern Vermont with my old friends Mary and Robert Houriet. Robert was writing a book about communes, *Getting Back Together*,* and I did his typing. He had spent more than two years preparing the book, including eight months on the road. One day a visitor asked him what the main conversational topic on the communes he'd visited had been. Perhaps he expected the answer

*Coward, McCann & Geoghegan, 1971.

13

to be "God," or "sex," or even "the political and economic situation." But Robert unhesitatingly answered, "Food."

I had earned my traveling money by working in New York as a live-in maid and cook for a Park Avenue lady. (It was a wonderful job; she found it endlessly amusing to have a maid who had gone to Bryn Mawr and was planning to write a commune cookbook.) At the end of May I set out on the road myself. First I hitched to California, then up through Oregon to British Columbia; returning to California, I took a circuitous route to New Mexico, recrossed the Midwest, circled Lake Superior, and reached New England via Canada. In five months I touched at forty-three communes and communities, staying anywhere from an hour to a week.

The people I met were kind, open, encouraging—and more. I am a food person who likes to talk about food the way bikers like to talk about motorcycles or astrology freaks about rising signs. Everywhere I went I found a passionate concern with food, what it tastes like, what it does for you. Both the art of cooking and the science of natural diet fascinated commune people, homesteaders, fellow hitchhikers, even the people who gave me rides. I was utterly gratified, understood; my notebooks filled. I returned to Vermont with news of a New Age of Food Consciousness.

This surge of interest is no coincidence. Desire for a purer diet is one of the main reasons why so many continue to "get it together and split for the country." If you want to eat organically grown food—that is, food not chemically fertilized, sprayed or processed—you almost have to grow your own. No one takes food for granted on a rural commune which farms, cooks and eats together. The garden itself is all the raison d'être

a commune needs, while dinner is the major event of its
day. Vegetables are one pillar of the commune diet.
The other, often bought in bulk through food co-ops run
by local longhairs, is grains. These simple ingredients
are served in unusual combinations, flavored with a
free hand by stoned culinary adventurers. Their
recipes are of unlimited interest.

Commune cooking is as variegated as a patchwork
quilt. I gathered Mexican, East Indian, Japanese,
Chinese, Tibetan, Israeli, Turkish, Armenian, North
African, Ugandian, Italian, Danish, Swedish, Jewish,
Hungarian, Russian, English and American Indian
recipes—as well as spontaneous inventions. I met
followers of the macrobiotic school (although its
popularity seemed to be waning, perhaps because it
tends toward drabness), Arnold Ehret's mucusless diet
(p. 145), Adelle Davis (whose emphasis on meat has
unfortunately lost her some of her commune following).
Certain ingredients and techniques, however, con-
sistently reappeared. The *sine qua non* of commune
cooking is tamari soy sauce, an unspeakably delicious
fermented Japanese product available in natural foods
stores which bears no resemblance to commercial soy
sauce.* Garlic is another constant, as are cider
vinegar, lemon juice, sea and sesame salt, sesame and
sunflower seeds, herbs, spices, honey instead of sugar,
oil instead of solid fats, whole wheat flour instead of
white. Chinese stir-frying (p. 20) is by far the preferred
method of preparing vegetable dishes.

Communes themselves are as uniquely seasoned as
their recipes. They are circles within a circle: extended families whose first point of reference is the
natural cycle of the year. Members look within the first

*Kikkoman soy sauce, available in supermarkets, tastes like tamari but
contains a preservative.

circle for entertainment. They read, discuss ideas, hold saunas, play guitars, drums, recorders, flutes, horns, fiddles, mouth harps. Festivals punctuate the year. The planting season begins with a celebration of the spring equinox, at which several communes may gather to make music, dance, trip and feast. The garden is often planted with accompanying ceremonies in emulation of the American Indians, whose spare, organic way of life has made them the heroes of country freaks. For the summer solstice, when lettuce and chard are being harvested in many regions and huge, pristine salads are consecrated by consumption every night, another party. The garden is a vegetable supermarket by the autumnal equinox, when the advent of chilly weather begins to weed out summer trippers. Now the core family can settle in for the winter. With so many to share the work, no one need be oppressed; when a group is drawn together by similar feelings about life, no one need be lonely.

Breakfast may be prepared by each individual as he straggles into the communal kitchen from his room or house or tepee or dome; lunch is haphazard; the meal on most communes is dinner. Most often it is prepared by two or three people, who are as likely to be men as women. This takes hours. Hungry members, drifting in, respond to the cooking smells with half-closed eyes and moans of pleasure. "You know it's right," Judith of High Ridge Farm, the illustrator for this book, writes of a recipe, "when everyone in the kitchen comes by all the time to take fingerfuls to taste."

The food is then laid out on a long table or perhaps on the ground with the group seated cross-legged around it: salad, a grain dish, one or two vegetable dishes, bread, an herbal tea, goat's milk, fruit, but so inventively prepared that each dinner seems like a feast. Before eating, everyone holds hands for a few minutes to chant "om," recite prayers of thanks or remain silent and gather his energies inward. Then the meal is eaten with full attention and enjoyment. Dishes may be a jumble of plates from sources as numerous as the family (on the average twelve to sixteen adults and several children, fewer in the winter) or hand-hewn wooden bowls. Chopsticks are offered along with the silverware.

This is a natural foods cookbook, with lapses. Unlike many, it does not attempt to be authoritative. The commune cooks and assorted freaks it represents differ widely in their attitudes. And then, how could you write a definitive commune cookbook? The movement itself is a retreat from rigidity. However, I have altered many of the recipes for publication. Since commune cooks rarely measure, I've had to establish exact amounts, using my own tastes as a guide. I've also set certain standards. Unadulterated canned goods like black olives and tomato paste are used, but processed products, white flour (even unbleached, which has still been stripped of most of its nutrients) and solid sugars (except in fermented beverages) are not.

It's a delightful joke on the press, I think, that most rural "hippie communes" should prove to be centered not on lurid sex or violent politics but on food. This is a cookbook to read with a light heart and a taste for high flavor. Commune recipes, like health, fresh air and hearty appetite, are for everyone. Savor them, whoever you are.

A Rap About Kitchen Tools

Kitchens everywhere are sympathetic places, but commune kitchens, rough-hewn, untidy and open, possess a special quality. Spend an hour in one, and sooner or later almost every member will have wandered in to prepare a snack or see who else is around. A long-skirted lady or bearded man may be kneading bread; the flour was probably ground in that quintessential commune appliance, a hand-powered grain mill. (About half the communes I visited had electricity, but its uses were usually limited to running a few lights, a pump, a battered stereo, perhaps a blender or a freezer to preserve garden produce.) Cooking is done on a wood stove. Overhead hang bunches of dried herbs, to be used for flavoring and in herbal teas. Culinary tools are ranged along the walls or sprout in profusion from coffee cans. Some of these are especially useful.

First, the *garlic press*. You'll notice that the recipes which follow call for quantities of garlic, and in every case I specify that it is to be mashed. Aside from being a tedious chore, mincing garlic leaves most of the cell walls intact. A garlic press efficiently breaks down cell walls to release the pungent oils within. The best press has a cylindrical chamber for the garlic clove; a cheaper, more common type has a horseshoe-shaped chamber which tends to let garlic escape around the plunger.

Instead of electric mixers, commune cooks use *whisks*. One type is round with a wire spiral around it; another is a coil on a handle (fun to bounce on the table). The best design, however, is a French whisk (pictured, p. 184), unparalleled for beating egg whites or unlumping sauces.

Although commune cooks usually throw ingredients together with intuitive boldness, some still prefer to measure, especially when preparing pastries. *Nested measuring cups* are especially helpful for this. You dip the cup into the flour or whatever and run a knife across the top. Only in this way can you be sure your measurements are exact. The margin of error when you use a liquid measuring cup to measure dry ingredients can run to several tablespoons.

The baking recipes have been tested without sifting the flours. However, I recommend sifting noninstant dry milk and carob powder to remove lumps. The best *sifter*, unaccountably hard to find, is the canister type with a hoop inside. I don't have one, so I do my sifting through a large sieve (another indispensable piece of equipment).

A *large serrated knife*—the type with tiny teeth—is excellent for slicing bread and juicy fruits like tomatoes and peaches. The teeth bite into the surface, then work their way through the soft inside without hacking, tearing or squishing.

The best type of *grater*, I've found, is the four-sided standing kind. I've often grated my knuckles on flat ones, which are difficult to hold. (Incidentally, if you place a standing grater over a candle in a dark room, you get wonderful dancing patterns.)

Tasting from the pot to correct the seasoning is essential to the art of cooking. At one commune, everyone gets stoned before dinner and seasons the main dish as a group. *Wooden spoons*, which don't conduct heat, allow you to taste without burning your tongue. Since they are porous, though, they do retain flavors, so don't mix up a cake with one that's been standing in a pot of spaghetti sauce.

I saw with my very own eyes, at a local discount house, an import from Japan labeled "Remon Squeezer." It was of the two-handled type; you put half a lemon inside and close it up. I prefer the type of *juicer* that's a dish with a ridged hemisphere inside to put the lemon or orange half on. You turn to extract the juice, then strain it. Citrus pulp contains factors called bioflavinoids, apparently important to the utilization of vitamin C, so it should not be discarded from juice to be drunk. Lemon juice for use in cooking, however, should be strained to remove the seeds.

My most useful utensil is my *wok*. It's a shallow, bowl-shaped Oriental skillet perfectly designed for stir-frying: its smooth sides facilitate ceaseless movement of chopped foods—the basis of Chinese cooking. The wok* comes with a ring, on which you set it over a high flame. (On a wood stove you may remove the stove lid and set the wok right into the hole.) First get the wok hot; then add oil and the food to be cooked at the same time. Stir-fry for only a few minutes, leaving the food still crisp. An iron wok will conduct heat better than an aluminum one. To keep it from rusting, rub it with salad oil after each use. Woks may be found at Oriental stores (but avoid cheap ones; a good wok should cost upwards of $13), fine department stores, Whole Earth truck stores or through the *Whole Earth Catalog*. I also have a wok spoon, a large thing like a slightly pointy hoe bent flat, that keeps the vegetables flying.

*There is an excellent discussion of woks and stir frying in *The Last Whole Earth Catalog*, Portola Institute/Random House, 1971, p. 196.

Aside from a wok, you should have at least one or two *cast-iron skillets*. These conduct heat evenly, without scorching. In particular, never cook milk-based dishes (like custard or pudding) or any bean dish in a thin saucepan. They burn readily and take on a vile flavor.

Of all culinary habits, the most rewarding to develop is that of storing foods well covered. Plastic wrap is efficient, but expensive and wasteful of non-renewable resources. Recycle plastic bags of all sorts, such as

plastic garment bags from the dry cleaners. Cover dishes with saucers (an obvious trick). Save all jars to store leftovers in. Foods stored covered and kept cool retain their vitamins best and don't end by being thrown away in disgust.

Useful Methods

How to chop an onion:

Bear in mind that an onion is composed of many layers which make the job of chopping it quite simple. Slice off the stem at the top and the furry root at the bottom. Slice it in half from stem to root (rather than through the equator). Remove the skin and the outer layer if it looks at all brown—if so, it will be tough. Place the onion halves cut side down on a chopping board. With a sharp knife, cut each half in slices 1/4 to 1/2 inch thick, first lengthwise and then across. You will have little squares that readily separate in cooking.

How to measure honey or molasses:

Cookbooks often tell you to grease your measuring cup or spoon before measuring honey or molasses. I've found that oiling the cup is more efficient. Pour oil into the measuring cup or spoon; swish it around; then pour it back into the oil container. Now measure the honey or molasses. It will slither right out of the cup without sticking.

How to peel a chili pepper:

There are several kinds of chili peppers: red, large green, small green. Red chilies are milder than green ones. Out West, large green chilies are commonly found; they are fairly mild. In New York, the only kind I've been able to locate is the small, hotter green chili. In the recipes that follow, you may use either a large or a small one when a green chili is specified, since the greater size of the former compensates for its mildness. The seeds are the hottest part of a chili, so include them if you have a taste for fiery food, omit them if you can't take it.

To peel chilies, you may oil them and put them under the broiler. Turn them every few minutes until they are black and blistered. Wrap them in a wet towel to cool down; then peel. If you are anxious to remove all seeds, wash the chili after peeling and deseeding. Do not touch any part of your face while peeling, and especially avoid touching your eyes. The chilies contain an irritating oil, which must be thoroughly washed away with hot water and soap after you finish.

Lisa of New Mexico (p. 74) has a different system. She suggests heating oiled chilies in a pan on top of the stove until they blister. Wrap in a towel as above; then peel with just your fingertips, scraping the seeds out with a spoon.

How to peel vegetables:

Don't if you can help it. The nutrients lie concentrated close to the skin, and furthermore, the peel usually adds flavor.

How to chop parsley, herbs and dried fruit:

Snip with a pair of scissors. Parsley, when called for

in this book, will be specified "snipped," since I'm convinced that's the best way to deal with it. Dried fruit like dates are also more easily snipped than chopped, but wash your scissors clean of the sugars that will cling to them afterward.

How to bake a pie shell:
When a recipe calls for a prebaked pie shell, my friend Mary lines the shell with oiled brown paper, then fills it with oiled dried beans, which hold the crust's shape during baking. The beans will be unharmed, although the oil coating will tend to make them cook a little more slowly than otherwise. Mary kept some soldier beans for years specifically for baking in pie shells, until a visitor accidentally cooked them.

How to get a wood stove hot:
I still haven't learned how to regulate our wood stove's oven well, but Mary figured out a system for making it good and hot: Get a fire going, close the damper on the stovepipe, close down the back draft (if you have one), and open the side draft up. The lower draft keeps the fire burning hotly, while the closed draft and damper hold the heat in.

A note about deep-frying in unrefined oil:
Some types of unrefined oil foam when heated and so are unsuitable for deep-frying. I've been told peanut oil is the only type of unrefined oil that won't foam. However, the soy oil I use doesn't foam either. Test your oil for foaming before attempting to deep-fry in it.
Most unrefined oils (corn, peanut, sesame, safflower) have characteristic flavors. Not all are suitable for

every purpose. Experiment until you find a type you like.

A note about dissolving yeast:

Adding honey to the water in which you dissolve your yeast gets yeast-risen doughs off to a racing start. I have recommended using powdered yeast for convenience, but many organic cooks prefer cake yeast. Sprinkle or crumble yeast into warm water in which you have dissolved a small amount of honey. Water should be quite warm—120° to 125°—for instant dry yeast, 115° for granular dry yeast, a little cooler for cake yeast. If the water is so hot that it hurts your submerged finger after a few seconds, it's too hot and will kill the yeast. One good idea is to practice taking the temperature of water with a thermometer to become familiar with how it feels to your finger at the correct heat. The yeast mixture should begin to foam several minutes after you add it to the water and honey and in five to ten minutes can be added to the other ingredients without stirring. If it doesn't foam, perhaps it's too old or you've inadvertently killed it.

A note about seasoning:

I tested the recipes in this book with powdered thyme. If you are using whole thyme leaves instead, you will probably want to add a bit more to compensate for their less concentrated flavor.

I. Soups

The commune soups I sampled were typically of mixed vegetables with a tomato or miso (p. 159) base, flavored with herbs. One excellent pre-harvest soup at Crow Farm in Oregon was made from vegetables thrown out by a local supermarket—although the loss of vitamins from elderly vegetables, not to mention their nonorganic origin, makes this a less than ideal source. I was served enough bland vegetarian pea soups to conclude that underseasoned pea soup, along with rancid oil, was a major commune problem. One young man who gave me a lift in California suggested flavoring pea soup with garlic and oregano and adding a few ounces of cream cheese at the end. You can also use tomato juice in whole or part as the liquid.

The soups below, all delicious and unusual, are not your run-of-the-mill commune soups.

Grady's Vegetable Soup

I met Grady, a slight, bearded artist, at Peter Gray's Valley in New Mexico. Just a few days earlier, masked gunmen had invaded his home in Santa Fe and taken sixty dollars. When a neighbor became involved in a shootout with the robbers, three men were wounded. Grady split to the quiet of the mountains to recover his peace of mind.

½ cup barley
½ cup pinto or other dry
    beans, soaked overnight
2 quarts beef or vegetable
    broth
1 large (28-ounce) can
    tomatoes, undrained
2 onions, chopped
2 to 4 cloves garlic, mashed
2 carrots, thinly sliced
    (see note)
1 potato, diced

1 teaspoon cumin
1 teaspoon oregano
½ teaspoon ginger
½ teaspoon turmeric
1 medium zucchini or yellow
    squash, thinly sliced
Corn scraped from 4 ears
    (raw or cooked) or a
    1-pound can of corn
2 cups chopped cabbage
¼ cup snipped parsley
Salt and pepper

Simmer barley and beans in broth for an hour and a half. Add tomatoes, onions, garlic, carrots, potato, herbs and spices, and simmer another hour. Add squash, corn, cabbage and parsley, and simmer another half hour. Salt and pepper to taste. This soup, like others of its type, is mellower next day.

Note: Grady suggests you add the carrot tops, finely chopped or snipped, along with the last vegetables.

Black Bean Soup

After a summer-long deluge, I was informed, Calabash Farm in southern Vermont had decided to call a moratorium on visitors. But there I was, pack and all, stranded and asking only for recipes, so they let me stay. The intimate commune of writers—five women and one man—shared a rambling farmhouse. I had a pleasant time and left the next day, so as not to strain my tenuous welcome. Blanche, a gentle-voiced, pretty lady from South Carolina who was learning wiring so she could install an electric heating system, drove me to the highway. "You know, yesterday I thought you might be a police agent," she remarked.

"If you ask me directly if I'm an agent, I have to answer, or my testimony won't be valid," I said.

There was a silence. Finally Blanche said, "Well, are you an agent?"

"No."

Another embarrassed silence followed as we approached the interstate entrance, then laughter and a good-bye accompanied by an embrace.

This Lebanese family recipe was brought by Kathy to Calabash from a commune in California.

1 cup black beans (see note)	2 to 4 cloves garlic, mashed
1 cup chick-peas	½ cup olive oil
1 cup lentils	Salt and pepper
½ teaspoon caraway seeds	2 onions, minced
½ cup brown rice	

Soak black beans and chick-peas overnight in water to cover. Do not drain. In the morning, put in a large pot with lentils, caraway seeds and 12 cups (3 quarts) water. Bring water to a boil, reduce heat, and simmer several hours, or until all are tender. Add water as necessary, maintaining a thick but soupy texture.

Cook rice separately in 1-1/4 cups water. Sauté onions and garlic in olive oil until browned. Add rice and onion mixture to the beans. Simmer 15 minutes. Season with salt and pepper to taste.

Note: Black beans are not the easiest thing in the world to locate. In New York, I searched for them in vain, only to find them at last in the Puerto Rican foods section of my local supermarket.

Beer Cheese Soup

In the dinner circle at Atlantis (p. 49), I remarked that I was apprehensive of visiting Crow Farm (p. 215) because of its reputation as a gang of lecherous beer drinkers. "You can go with me," the girl beside me said softly. "I live there sometimes. I want to go anyway, and I don't like to hitchhike alone because I'm only twelve."

"What!" I exclaimed, and stared at her. I had taken her for eighteen; but when I looked closely, her face slipped into focus, and I saw it was true.

The next day we left, she carrying a sack of keepsakes instead of gear. On the way we stopped off at another of her part-time homes, a communal house in Eugene. Her parents were divorced; her father lived down in California, her mother and baby brother in a collective elsewhere in the city. Quiet, shy, a constant but not precocious reader, the girl wandered unobtrusively among several communes. The adults in this disorganized but friendly house were kind to her in an offhand way and put me up for several days. The recipe below was given to me here by Robin, a poet.

3 cups beef broth, vegetable broth or water
2 potatoes, finely grated
2 carrots, finely grated
1 onion, finely grated
2 to 3 cloves garlic, mashed
1 to 2 cups (¼ to ½ pound)

grated sharp cheese
1 12-ounce can (1½ cups) beer (see note)
1 tablespoon tamari
½ teaspoon salt
¼ teaspoon black pepper

Heat broth to boiling. Add grated vegetables and garlic. Reduce heat, and simmer 30 minutes. Add beer and cheese, stirring until cheese melts. Cover, and simmer a few minutes. Add tamari, salt and pepper. This soup tastes rather like a cheese fondue.

Note: You may add 1/4 pound sliced mushrooms, sautéed in 2 tablespoons butter or oil, along with the beer and cheese.

Toog-Pah

Milkweed Hill in Vermont supports itself by a candlemaking operation carried on in a geodesic dome. Lorraine, a member, had been described to me by friends who had visited the backwoods commune as an herbwoman and a witch. Dressed in an ankle-length gown, she tenderly wheedled her crying baby into silence so we could talk. She was tall and had a habit, which I found endearing, of leaning up very close to me as we talked. Later I learned that she was very nearsighted and had decided to do without her glasses.

(There's a belief current among freaks that willpower and exercises can compensate for poor vision.) Lorraine let me copy recipes from a notebook she'd kept for years of her own and friends' inventions. I told her she'd amazed me with her generosity. She laughed. "One witch knows another when they meet," she said.

Lorraine attributed this soup to Tibetan origins. Since then a friend just back from Nepal has explained that *toog-pah* is a generic term there for noodle soup.

2 tablespoons oil
¼ teaspoon cayenne
¼ teaspoon black pepper
1 teaspoon ginger
3 to 4 cloves garlic, mashed
1 pound lean lamb, diced
1 tablespoon whole wheat flour
¼ cup tamari
6 cups water
2 carrots, diced
2 stalks celery, diced

2 onions, chopped
1 cup cabbage, chopped
6 tomatoes, quartered, or
    1-pound can of tomatoes,
    undrained
1 green pepper, chopped
1 cup sprouts
1 recipe for Whole Wheat
    Noodles (opposite)
Salt

Heat oil in a kettle. Add spices and garlic, and sauté several minutes over medium heat. Add lamb, and sear well. Then add flour, and stir. Add remaining ingredients except sprouts, noodles and salt and bring to a boil. Lower heat, and simmer 10 minutes.

Meanwhile, prepare Whole Wheat Noodles (opposite). Bring 2 quarts water to a boil in a large saucepan, and slowly add the noodles. Cook 5 minutes over high heat, stirring often to prevent the noodles from sticking to each other. Drain.

Add noodles and sprouts to the soup, and heat 1 more minute. Salt to taste.

Whole Wheat Noodles

¾ cup whole wheat flour   1 egg
½ teaspoon salt   1 tablespoon water

Combine flour and salt. In a small bowl, beat egg and water until the egg is light. Stir in the flour and salt. Knead the dough for several minutes. You may simply manipulate it in your hand, since it is too small to knead on a surface as you do bread. Sprinkle a smooth surface generously with whole wheat flour and roll out the noodle dough very thin. Cut into very narrow strips about 2 inches long with a sharp knife.

Brotherhood Spirit in Flesh Soup

The Brotherhood of the Spirit is a cult located in a community in western Massachusetts. Led by a youthful guru who in turn receives spiritual teachings from a medium, a retired bus driver, the Brotherhood hopes to spread its message through a rock group called "Spirit in Flesh." This was the very first commune I ever visited, and it was a weird, yet encouraging experience. Everyone I met visibly throbbed with good vibes and energy. Several members came up to me to speak with deep concern about the spirit within me waiting to be released, staring unwaveringly into my eyes as they talked. By the kitchen door (beyond which visitors were not allowed), I told a young man about the book I'd just decided to do. I wanted to see if he'd take me seriously. He said he'd write down what they were making for dinner that night—he wouldn't know what it was until they'd made it. Later he handed me this. "Put that in your book," he said.

Get everyone together and get a good feeling between you. Work out anything and everything that lies unexpressed. Realize that you are *Spirit*–and that the health and balance of those you feed depend only on your *Thoughts*—that balance and order of the body depend on balance and order of the Mind Positive. The ingredients are of secondary importance, and always in a divine relativity. This soup was made by Alan, Martin, Tam, Lynne and others, and Duh Bear.

1. Two big pots half full of boiling water.
2. Add 2 cups of pinto beans and a little later several handfuls of barley.
3. To each then add a lot of sautéed onions. At this writing the soup isn't done, but we'll add 12 canning quarts of squash, carrots and tomatoes from last summer's garden. Also some green beans someone gave us. Later some salt and seasoning, kelp powder and a few tablespoons of miso to each. Follow your own *Awareness* most of all.

This soup will feed 130 along with two pots of brown rice and two pots of millet. Pots are about 3 or 4 gallons.

Finally, one last ingredient to be used throughout— *Love*.

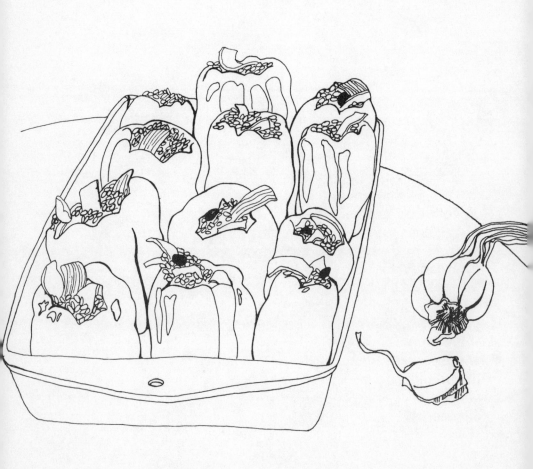

II. Vegetarian Main Dishes

This is the most valuable chapter in the book. Vegetables, grains and dairy products form the basis of the commune diet, and those who rely on nonmeat sources of protein will find these recipes particularly interesting. Commune people may detect a false note, however: An embarrassing percentage call for cheese, which is actually a luxury on many communes. Well, you gave me the recipes, brothers and sisters. The only thing I can think of to do about it is offer this advice to would-be commune visitors. Remember that you are intruding on a private family, make your stay brief, volunteer for unpopular jobs, and, above all, bring cheese.

Eggplant Spaghetti

Prairie Dog Village, one of the most charming communes I visited, occupied a defunct lumbering town in the redwood country of northern California. Members lived in the original sprawling houses, with interior partitions removed to create great spaces. A stream ran through the property in a deep, wooded glade. Over it had been built a teahouse, a sort of tree house open on all sides, with a hibachi on which to brew the tea. Even the floor of this airy little structure was open in the center, so you could look straight down into the brook. When you were alone there, the tinkling waters lulled you into a meditative trance.

"Oh, wow, you really came to the right place," Debbie told me when I arrived. "We're really into food here." Everyone took turns cooking in pairs, and worthwhile inventions were written down. This one is especially splendid. The eggplant cooks to a wonderful consistency with a meatlike richness.

½ cup oil
1 large eggplant, chopped
2 onions, chopped
8 cloves garlic, mashed
1 green pepper, chopped
1 carrot, chopped
2 large (28-ounce) cans tomatoes
1 15-ounce can tomato sauce
1 bay leaf
1 teaspoon each basil, oregano
½ teaspoon each marjoram,
rosemary, thyme
½ cup snipped parsley
1 cup red or white wine
½ head cauliflower,
finely chopped
¼ pound mushrooms, sliced
1 teaspoon salt
Wheat-soy or buckwheat
spaghetti
Parmesan cheese

In a large kettle, heat the oil over medium heat. Add eggplant, onions, garlic, green pepper, and carrot.

Sauté for 15 minutes, stirring. Add tomatoes, tomato sauce, herbs and parsley. Bring to a boil, reduce heat, and simmer 3 to 4 hours, gradually adding wine. Half an hour before it is done, add cauliflower and mushrooms. Salt at end. Serve with wheat-soy or buckwheat spaghetti and lots of Parmesan cheese. Serves 10 to 12. Even better the next day.

Sweet-and-Sour Spaghetti Sauce

A small boy at High Ridge Farm in Oregon was describing to several other children a home he'd visited with his parents. "They had spaghetti," he said, "and it was icky. And you know why it was icky? Because it had meat balls in it!"

2 tablespoons oil
2 onions, chopped
2 to 4 cloves garlic, mashed
2 tablespoons oil
1 large (28-ounce) can tomatoes
  or 12 ripe tomatoes,
  quartered
1 small (8-ounce) can
  tomato sauce
1 tablespoon cider vinegar
1 tablespoon honey

1 tablespoon tamari
¼ teaspoon thyme
½ teaspoon oregano
½ teaspoon dried
  dillweed or
  1½ teaspoons fresh
  snipped dill
2 tablespoons raisins
  or currants
1 cup (¼-pound) grated
  sharp cheese

Heat oil in a saucepan over medium heat. Sauté onions and garlic until browned. Add all ingredients except cheese. Heat till the mixture bubbles; then lower heat, and simmer 1 hour. Stir in cheese until it melts. Serve with wheat-soy or buckwheat spaghetti.

Eileen, Wheeler's Ranch, California

Stuffed Eggplant

Wheeler's Ranch, the highest place in California, is an open land community, not a commune. Lou Gottlieb, a successful jazz musician, began the open land movement when he deeded his Morningstar Ranch to God. Following his example, Bill Wheeler, an artist, "liberated" a large tract nearby in Sonoma County. Wheeler's Ranch, now incorporated for legal reasons as the Ahimsa Open Land Church, is home to whoever cares to find a vacant hut or build one. It's a strange and funny place. The dirt road in is as rutted as a riverbed, but you can't leave your car on the highway or local vigilantes will smash your windshield. Once the perilous mile in is negotiated, you may find nobody about, although the population must number well over a hundred. Everyone lives tucked away in little hobbit holes among the dense shrubbery, chiefly poison oak, where all subsist very simply on grains and vegetables or government commodities food. The most remote canyon shelters renegades who rarely leave it. Once two escapees from San Quentin came to live there. The authorities found out and moved in with several hundred men and a helicopter. They recaptured one of the convicts and took the opportunity to bust some of the inhabitants for growing dope. Nevertheless, the community still thrives despite continual harassment. It has only one rule. Some time ago the ranch dogs began to revert to their natural impulses and hunt in packs. After the sheep of neighboring farmers had been attacked, dogs were excluded. Now hundreds of cats roam the ranch in their stead.

Individuals live and cook separately, although there is a community garden, a ranch cow and every Sunday a "feast"—a plain but ample meal to which the world is invited. Eileen lives in a small, neat A-frame. She, Micheline (p. 180) and I sat up late one night fantasizing about food. Here is one of her recipes.

1 large unpeeled eggplant
2 tablespoons oil or butter
1 onion, chopped
2 gloves garlic, mashed
¼ cup cold cooked brown
   rice or other grain
2 slices whole wheat bread,

   crumbled
1 teaspoon basil
½ teaspoon salt
⅛ teaspoon black pepper
1 cup (¼-pound) grated
   sharp cheese
Parmesan cheese (optional)

In a large saucepan or kettle, bring 1 inch water to a boil. Add eggplant. Cover, lower heat, and simmer 30 minutes, turning once after 15 minutes. Remove from heat, and cool.

Cut eggplant in half. Remove the pulp, leaving a half-inch shell. Dice the meat. Place shells on a baking sheet or baking dish.

Preheat oven to 350°.

Heat oil or butter in a skillet over medium heat. Sauté onion and garlic several minutes. Add eggplant, and sauté, stirring, until tender. Add rice, bread, seasonings and sharp cheese. Mix well. Heap into eggplant shells, and sprinkle generously with Parmesan cheese if you wish. Bake 45 minutes. Serves 4.

Vegetable Curry

A brilliant invention of Debbie's, of Prairie Dog Village.

3 tablespoons oil
3 onions, halved and thinly sliced
3 cloves garlic, mashed
¼ pound mushrooms, sliced
2 stalks celery, chopped
1 cup broccoli, chopped

1 cup cauliflower, chopped
1 medium zucchini, sliced
4 teaspoons curry powder
2 teaspoons ginger
1/3 cup tamari
1 cup sour cream or yogurt
½ cup sesame seeds, toasted

Heat oil over medium heat in a saucepan or skillet. Add onions, garlic and mushrooms, and sauté several minutes. Add the other vegetables, and stir. Add spices and tamari, lower heat, and simmer 15 minutes. Fold in sour cream or yogurt, and simmer another 5 minutes. Sprinkle with sesame seeds. Serve with brown rice and Chutney (p. 228). Serves 4.

Darrel's Curry

High Ridge Farm in Oregon has an enduring quality. I can imagine the High Ridge family raising their children and growing old together. Two years ago, for moral reasons, the group decided to stop accepting food stamps. Hard times followed. Resourcefully, they took a disagreeable job doing farmwork, which they made bearable by rotating. Then a member unexpectedly received a substantial trust fund. Now the commune prospers. When I visited in June, I was reminded equally of the Garden of Eden and a summer camp.

The eighteen adult members seemed remarkably compatible in their values, interests, energies. Most paired in couples (like the majority of commune people I met), they lived scattered about the steeply sloping property in various idiosyncratic dwellings: large and small A-frames; an unfinished dome; a cabin adjoining a sauna. A new communal building was being constructed to replace the boxlike original farmhouse where meals were cooked and the children slept. An adult slept in with them every night, almost the only family routine. My first two nights, for example, I did the dishes, then decided to leave them for somebody else. They remained undone. It took all my self-control not to panic and wash them myself. Finally, the next morning, Claudia tackled them. Later I told Judith, the illustrator for this book, how I'd felt. She laughed at my fears and explained that they'd rather let the dishes sit in the sink than feel under compulsion to do them.

High Ridge Farm's gardens were extraordinary, partly owing to the work of a professional gardener in the family. Seedlings were started in a greenhouse. You could pluck the lavish strawberry bed bare one night and find it replete with ripe berries next morning. Cooking, like dishwashing, was usually volunteered for on impulse and ran to the experimental. Once before I prepared a dish, I asked Jean if she thought it would go over well. "Everyone likes everything here," she replied. The following is Darrel's creation. Coconut, sunflower seeds, raw peanuts and raisins are all staples at High Ridge.

2½ cups unsweetened coconut (see note)
4 cups water
2 onions, halved and thinly sliced
2 cloves garlic, mashed
2 tablespoons oil
1 tablespoon curry powder
1 teaspoon coriander
1 teaspoon turmeric
1 teaspoon cloves
1 teaspoon cinnamon
Dash cayenne
½ teaspoon tarragon
¼ teaspoon caraway seeds
1 teaspoon poppy seeds
1 bay leaf
2 tablespoons lemon juice
½ cup raisins or currants
½ cup dates, chopped
½ cup peanuts or other nuts, chopped
½ cup sunflower seeds

Cover 2 cups of the coconut with the water, and bring to a boil. Lower heat, and simmer 15 minutes. Pour into a large sieve or a double thickness of cheesecloth, and squeeze or press to extract all liquid. If you are patient and work with small amounts at a time, you will obtain considerably more liquid. Discard coconut. The chickens will like it.

In a large skillet, sauté onions and garlic in oil over medium heat. When lightly browned, add coconut water ("milk"). Stirring constantly, add remaining 1/2 cup coconut, spices, herbs and lemon juice. Lower heat, and simmer 15 minutes, stirring occasionally.

Add fruit, nuts and seeds, and cook another 5 minutes. Add water to thin to desired consistency. Serve over rice with fruit salad on the side and Chutney (p. 228). Serves 8.

Note: Unsweetened coconut is available at natural foods stores. If you use sweetened supermarket coconut, you'll sorely regret it—the curry will be disgustingly sweet.

My favorite accompaniment to curry is bananas, halved and cut into inch-long pieces, sautéed over medium heat for several minutes in a mixture of oil and butter.

Couscous

A version of the classical North African dish from Earth, Air, Fire and Water, a hardworking commune in northern Vermont that raises beef cattle and keeps a team of horses for field work.

1 cup chick-peas, soaked overnight
2½ cups water
1 bay leaf
4 tablespoons oil (¼ cup)
2 onions, chopped
2 to 4 cloves garlic, mashed
2 cups bulgur wheat or wheat berries cracked in a grain mill set on coarse grind
4 cups boiling water, broth,
or vegetable stock
4 to 5 cups raw vegetables, chopped (see note)
6 ripe tomatoes, quartered, or 1 1-pound can tomatoes, undrained
1 ½ teaspoons mixed herbs (see note)
3 tablespoons tamari
¼ teaspoon cayenne

In a saucepan, cover chick-peas with 2-1/2 cups water, including their soaking water. Add bay leaf. Bring to a boil, reduce heat, and simmer until tender, about 1-1/2 hours (3 hours if soaking has been omitted). Add water if necessary.

Heat 2 tablespoons oil (or butter) in a saucepan or skillet over medium heat, and sauté onions and garlic until brown. Add bulgur or cracked wheat, and brown a few more minutes. Pour in boiling liquid slowly, cover, and lower heat. Simmer until all liquid is absorbed and wheat is tender, about 20 minutes for bulgur, 30 minutes for cracked wheat. Keep warm.

Heat 2 tablespoons oil in a skillet or wok, and add vegetables, tomatoes and herbs. If you are using fresh

tomatoes, add them also; if canned, add later. Stir-fry
for several minutes over medium-high heat. If you are
using slower-cooking vegetables such as carrots or
cauliflower, you may cover the pan and steam them for
a few more minutes, or leave them crunchy.

Add chick-peas with their liquid, tamari and
cayenne to vegetables. Pour over the wheat. Serves 6.

Note: Good vegetables include zucchini, summer
squash, cabbage, peas, green beans, sprouts, broccoli,
mushrooms, carrots, cauliflower, celery, mushrooms,
green pepper.

Herbs may include basil, rosemary, oregano,
marjoram, savory, thyme, tarragon, sage, dillweed.
However, go lightly on the last four, as their flavors
easily predominate.

Chop Suey

During my idyl with the Furry Freak Brothers in New
Mexico (p. 83), word came that a baby was about to be
born nearby. Several members hurried off to be
present. A medical student who was spending the
summer at the commune suggested I go too. With no
premonition of the extraordinary experience I was to
have, I went. It was as if he had offered me a little
white pill of LSD and said, "Here, take this"—and with
no forethought I had.

The van had left, so I walked two miles to the highway down a dusty dirt road, past Chicano children
playing outside adobe houses and a little cemetery
whose graves were marked by metal crosses and

garish artificial flowers. At the blacktop, three women in a pickup truck stopped for me. They too were on their way to Karen and Baba's.

Karen's parents, who had come from suburban California, for the birth, had engaged a young, long-haired obstetrician to show Baba, a former member of the nearby Hog Farm commune, how to deliver his child. Twenty friends had also crowded into the sunny whitewashed adobe cottage. I felt out of place, knowing hardly anyone, and while we waited for the last period of labor to begin, I talked outside to a young man who also had never met the couple. He gave me the recipe below, invented at what he described as an impromptu commune in Aspen, Colorado, a popular summering place for freaks.

Sounds of jubilation pulled us into the bedroom for the final hour. I soon forgot I was a stranger. The group clustered around the bed cried out with each contraction, some chanting "om," some groaning in sympathy with Karen, whose lovely face screwed up with the effort. "When is it going to come?" she whimpered. Her mother stayed in the kitchen, smoking nervously, but sometimes her father came in and caressed the back of her head.

The contractions grew more and more intense. As the dark crown of the baby's head began to appear, our excitement rose, but each time Karen was given a mirror to look at herself, the head had disappeared. Suddenly with a last spasm the whole head emerged. The doctor moved in beside Baba and wrestled out the shoulders. Everyone responded with passionate cries. I was so unexpectedly moved that I burst into tears. Then as Karen received her wailing daughter into her

arms, she was given the astrological calculations:
Virgo, moon in Capricorn, Scorpio rising.

¼ cup tamari
½ teaspoon honey
¼ cup oil, preferably sesame
1 tablespoon arrowroot starch
   (see note)
1 cup broth, vegetable cooking
   water or vegetable boullion
½ teaspoon salt
¼ teaspoon black pepper
1 cup red or green cabbage,
   sliced

6 scallions, thinly sliced
1 onion, halved and thinly
   sliced
2 stalks celery, thinly sliced
1 medium zucchini or summer
   squash, thinly sliced
2 to 4 cloves garlic, mashed
1½ cups sprouts
1 green pepper, halved
   lengthwise and thinly sliced
Bulgur or brown rice

In one cup, combine tamari, honey and 2 tablespoons
of the oil. In a second, dissolve the arrowroot starch,
broth, cooking water or bouillon, salt and pepper.

Heat the rest of the oil in a wok, deep heavy skillet or
large saucepan over medium-high heat. Add the
cabbage, scallions, onion, celery, squash and garlic.
Stir-fry 3 minutes.

Add tamari mixture. Lower heat to medium, cover,
and steam 3 minutes.

Add arrowroot starch mixture. Stir over medium
heat until mixture thickens and boils.

Add sprouts and green peppers. Cover, lower flame,
and simmer two minutes. Serve with bulgur or brown
rice. Serves 4 to 6.

Note: Arrowroot starch is a natural substitute for
refined cornstarch, but in a pinch the latter may be
substituted.

You may also add a thinly sliced carrot along with
the first vegetables, or 1/4 pound mushrooms, sliced,
along with the sprouts and green pepper. Green beans
cut in inch lengths may be substituted for the sprouts,
but add them with the first vegetables.

Vegetable Hamburger

Grady (p. 28) suggested this convenient way to use leftover grains and cereals—even intransigent oatmeal. The flavoring is characteristically New Mexican. Grady's favorite way to serve the "hamburger" is in taco shells (p. 93) with lettuce, grated cheese and a chili sauce.

2 cups leftover grain (rice, millet, bulgur, cooked cereal, etc.)
1 onion, chopped
1 stalk celery, chopped
2 tablespoons chopped nuts
2 tablespoons sunflower seeds

1 to 2 eggs
1½ teaspoons chili powder
¼ teaspoon oregano
⅛ teaspoon cayenne
½ teaspoon salt (less if grain is salted)
2 tablespoons oil

Mix together all ingredients except oil. Heat oil in a skillet over medium heat, and fry mixture until brown, breaking it into crumbles with a fork. Use in any dish that calls for ground meat, such as enchiladas or chili con carne, adding at the last minute instead of at the time indicated in the recipe.

Ground Nut Stew

Inspired by a vision of love and brotherhood, Atlantis, in Oregon, is dedicated to the principle of open community. When I visited, a year after it was founded, this place where none was turned away had become a stop on the commune-hopping circuit. At its center, a small committed group was earnestly attempting to center a real community on the one permanent structure, a battered farmhouse. Around them swirled a constantly fluctuating population of tran-

sients who sometimes contributed, sometimes in-
terfered. One loud middle-aged man had made himself
indispensable with gifts of cash; when he heard about
my book, he offered me money, too, just in case I
needed it.

The ceremony before dinner and, unprecedently,
even breakfast was very elaborate. The food was
placed on the floor, and the group sat around it in a
circle, holding hands. First we chanted "om" for a few
minutes and recited the Lord's Prayer. Then several
members recited another prayer. It went: "From the
point of light within the mind of God, let light stream
forth into the hearts of men. May Christ return to earth
from the center, where the will of God is known. Let
purpose guide the little wills of men, the purpose which
the masters know and serve. From the center, which
we call the family, the race of man, let the plan of love
and light work on. And may it seal the door where evil
dwells. Let light and love and power restore the plan
on earth. Om shanti."

At last the food was passed around, including, as a
special treat, a magnificent fruit salad. Some people
heaped their plates high with the fruit salad, while
others at the far end got none. "There's no room for
selfishness in a family of forty," one of the most
dedicated members half admonished, half pleaded.
"Those who took too much should put some back." The
offenders sullenly continued eating, ignoring the glares
they received. At last, since nobody was willing to
make a heavy scene, those who hadn't got fruit salad
made do with beans.

Atlantis may find it has to close its doors to survive,
or it may become the Wheeler's Ranch of Oregon: a

sanctuary for both the gentle and the lunatic, kept viable by separate living arrangements and a shared belief in the ultimate rightness of the Flow, whether it brings good or evil. Meanwhile, Atlantis trucks on. The central group had prepared a comic book, which it hoped to have published by an underground press, telling the story of the commune and describing its vision of a better, more brotherly world. It included a number of original quantity recipes such as Millet Balls, Yogurt Divinity Deluxe and Atlantis Dream Candy Bars. Here is a scaled-down version of a Ugandian stew. Authentically, the recipe ends, "Eat with fingers."

3 tablespoons oil
2 onions, chopped
4 cloves garlic, mashed
2 carrots, diced
½ head cauliflower, chopped
6 ripe tomatoes, quartered,
  or 1-pound can tomatoes,
  undrained

1 cup raw unsalted peanuts
  in their jackets, chopped
½ cup peanut butter
½ cup water
1 teaspoon chili powder
⅛ teaspoon cayenne
Salt
Cooked rice or steamed millet

Heat oil in a skillet over medium heat. Brown onions and garlic. Add carrots and cauliflower, and sauté several more minutes. Add tomatoes, cover, lower heat, and simmer one-half hour.

Stir in peanuts, peanut butter and water, and add seasonings. Amount of salt will depend on the saltiness of the type of peanut butter you use. To get the benefit of the unsaturated oils in peanuts, you should use only the unhydrogenated kind—you can tell if it's good by whether it separates or not, since hydrogenation solidifies the oil so it won't rise. Serve with rice, or to be more African, steamed millet. Serves 4 to 6.

Total Loss Spinach Blintzes

I arrived at every commune high on the hope of collecting the ultimate recipe. At Total Loss Farm, the Vermont commune made famous by Ray Mungo, I greeted Richard with "Hi! I'm writing a commune cookbook!" He smiled mysteriously. "So are we," he replied. His family even had a contract, unlike me. We sat around in the kitchen and talked obliquely for an hour. "We eat really well here," Richard remarked. "Last week we had spinach blintzes." I cheered up. "Really? How did you make them? Are you going to have them in your book?" They weren't, so here is my conception of what they ate.

1 recipe Swedish Pancakes (p. 166) Sour cream or yogurt
  omitting the vanilla   2 tablespoons oil or
½ pound spinach   1 tablespoon oil and
1 cup cottage, farmer or feta   1 tablespoon butter
  cheese   Sour cream or yogurt
Salt and pepper

Prepare 1 recipe Swedish Pancakes in a small skillet. You should have about 12 pancakes. Cook them only on one side, removing them carefully when bubbles appear. Set them on dampened paper towels or dish towels to keep them from sticking to each other. (I used plain white typing paper, which I dipped in water.)
FILLING: Wash spinach and place in a saucepan with a lid. Set over medium flame, and steam for several minutes in the water that clings to the leaves, or until wilted. Chop spinach and combine, with its liquid, with the cheese and salt and pepper to taste.
TO ASSEMBLE: Place about 2 rounded tablespoons of the mixture on each pancake. Roll up, and fold under at the ends. Have the oil or oil mixture heated in a skillet, and as each blintz is ready, pop it into the skillet,

folded side down. Cook over medium heat until golden brown, turning once. Keep finished blintzes warm in a low oven until all are ready. Serve with sour cream or yogurt. Serves 4.

Spinach Pudding

Nuns at a neighboring convent gave this recipe to Carleen of Prairie Dog Village, in northern California.

1 pound spinach (a bucketful)	½ cup grated Cheddar or
2 eggs	Jack cheese
2 cups cottage cheese	Parmesan cheese

Preheat oven to 350°.

Wash the spinach, and put it in a pot with a lid. Place over medium heat, and steam several minutes in the water that clings to its leaves, until wilted. You may chop the leaves, for bite-size pieces, or leave them whole.

Beat the eggs, and combine with the cottage cheese and grated cheese. Add the spinach and its juices. Pour into a well-oiled baking or soufflé dish. Top with a good sprinkling of Parmesan. Bake for half an hour, or until puffy and brown. Serves 4.

Armenian Polenta

This recipe originates with a mustached man who gave me a ride from the frying pan of open land communities, Wheeler's Ranch, to the fire, Morningstar Ranch, eight miles away. He was one of countless graduate students in sociology preparing a master's thesis on the counterculture. I asked him how

he did his research. "I go to bars and talk to freaks,"
he said. "But they don't like me."

1 recipe for Corn Bread (p. 179), using 3 cups milk	4 green chilies, peeled and chopped (p. 23)
1-pound can corn, drained, or corn cut from 4 ears, cooked	1 cup (¼-pound) grated Cheddar cheese

Preheat oven to 350°.

Prepare Corn Bread, doubling the liquid as indicated. Oil a medium casserole dish well. Pour in one-
third of the corn bread batter. On top of that, sprinkle
half the corn, half the chopped green chilies and half
the grated cheese. Top with another third of the batter,
and sprinkle with the rest of the other ingredients. Top
with the last third of the batter. Cover and set in a
warm place to rise 30 to 45 minutes. Bake 35 to 40
minutes, or until a knife comes out clean. Serves 8.

Mexican-Italian Goulash

I found this recipe written out on a slip of paper
stashed among the cookbooks at Atlantis, in Oregon.
(All communes have a shelf of cookbooks, ranging from
Cosmic Cookery and *The Tassajara Bread Book* to *The
Fannie Farmer Cookbook*, with *The Joy of Cooking* the
overwhelming favorite. They also have several junked
cars in front, two or more large barking dogs, with
German shepherds and black mongrels predominating,
and a cat with kittens.) Containing no measurements, it
had the ring of originality. Perhaps someday the in-
ventor will be manifested to me (see Judy's Honey
Wine, p. 220).

4 ripe tomatoes, cut up
1 small can ripe olives,
    pitted and halved
2 green chilies, skinned
    and chopped (p. 23)
½ cup sliced mushrooms (see note)

1 teaspoon oregano or basil
½ teaspoon salt
2 cloves garlic, mashed
1 cup (¼-pound) sharp
    cheese, grated

Place all ingredients in a cold skillet. Place over a low flame, and heat, stirring, until the cheese melts. Serve with Mexican Rice:

2 tablespoons butter or oil
1 onion, chopped
1 clove garlic, crushed
1 cup brown rice
2½ cups boiling water

1 teaspoon curry powder
⅛ teaspoon cayenne
Pinch saffron (optional)
1 teaspoon salt

Heat oil or butter in a skillet or saucepan, and sauté onion and garlic for several minutes over medium heat. Add rice, and sauté several more minutes. Add water and spices, stir to combine, cover, lower heat, and simmer 50 minutes, or until rice is tender. Serves 4.

Note: You may sauté the mushrooms first in 2 tablespoons butter for additional flavor.

Atlantis, Oregon

Peanut Rice

This splendid, unlikely melding of flavors and textures also combines two incomplete proteins to form a complete protein (p. 111).*

3 tablespoons oil, preferably
    peanut
2 onions, chopped
2 to 4 cloves garlic, mashed
1 cup unsalted raw peanuts

    in their jackets
3 cups cold cooked brown
    rice
2 tablespoons tamari
¼ teaspoon cayenne

*A recent cookbook, *Diet for a Small Planet*, by Frances Moore Lappé (Ballantine), explores this question extensively.

Heat oil over medium heat, and sauté onions and garlic until browned. Add peanuts, and sauté several more minutes, stirring often. Then add rice, and sauté several more minutes, stirring. Season. Serves 4.

Bibs Family, Vermont

Falafel

A sign at the entrance to the Goat Farm in Oregon reads WELCOME BACK TO EARTH, and another, in the vegetable patch, BLESS THIS GARDEN. I watched one member trim the hooves of several goats from the commune's herd of fourteen. Goats that don't have a chance to clamber on rocky surfaces get "ingrown hooves" if the excess growth isn't pared away periodically, he explained. A few hundred yards from the rickety farmhouse where the youthful group of twelve lived, two families had raised tepees. I took a picture of three children with long blond braids outside their tepee, maundering on about how sweet the little girls looked. "But we're little boys," one of them piped. Blushing, I returned to the farmhouse, where Eileen, a dynamic young woman, had organized a team to prepare falafel. She had learned how to make this eastern Mediterranean specialty on an Israeli kibbutz. "It was the only interesting thing we ever ate," she remarked.

Prepare the pita bread first, then while it rises make the sauce and the falafel mixture. While the bread bakes, fry the falafel balls.

PITA BREAD:

1½ cups warm water
1 teaspoon honey
1 package yeast

3 cups whole wheat flour
1½ teaspoons salt

Pour the water into a bowl and dissolve the honey. Sprinkle in the yeast. Allow to stand until active (p. 25). Combine flour and salt. Stir into the liquid and knead until thoroughly blended—about 100 times. Form into 12 balls. Let rest 5 minutes; then roll each ball out with a rolling pin into a circle 5 inches across. Place on two oiled baking sheets and turn over to oil tops. Set in a warm place and allow to rise one hour.

Heat over to 450°. Bake the pita loaves 12 to 15 minutes, or until lightly browned. Pita bread is supposed to puff up and form a pocket in the middle. It never has yet for me, but these loaves are capacious and tasty.

SAUCE:

1½ cups well-cooked chick-peas (2/3 cup uncooked)
½ cup chick-pea cooking water
2 to 3 cloves garlic, mashed

1 tablespoon oil
2 tablespoons tamari
3 tablespoons tahini (see note) or ground sesame seeds

Mash chick-peas with a potato masher, fork or the back of a slotted spoon. Blend the other ingredients. (Or place all ingredients in a blender and whir. If you are using sesame seeds, include them whole, to be ground in the blender, but make your tablespoons heaping to compensate for the loss of volume in grinding.)

FALAFEL BALLS:

3 cups cooked chick-peas (1 1/3 cups raw)
¼ cup whole wheat flour
2 tablespoons tamari
1 egg

1½ teaspoons chili powder
⅛ teaspoon cayenne
2 cloves garlic, mashed
Peanut oil

Mash the chick-peas as above. Blend in other ingredients except oil.

Over medium-high heat, heat 1/2 inch peanut oil (other types of unrefined oil will foam) in a skillet. Form falafel mixture into balls the size of large marbles. Fry in oil a few at a time until browned. Remove with a slotted spoon and keep warm in a low oven until all are done.

TO ASSEMBLE: Set out salad ingredients such as shredded lettuce, chopped ripe tomato and minced scallion. Split leaves, and fill with several falafel balls, salad and sauce. Eat like a sandwich, holding over a plate to catch the delicious drip. Serves 8.

Note: Tahini, or sesame puree, is available in natural foods stores.

Curried Squash and Chick-peas

The Woolman Hill School in Massachusetts is a free school whose only links with tradition are the tuition and board charges to parents that support it. (A similar irony: after a number of unsuccessful culinary experiments, The Theatre of All Possibilities, a group in New Mexico, reportedly made a rule that all cooking was to be done from cookbooks.) The afternoon I arrived, someone was complaining that there was nothing for dinner but squash and chick-peas. So I invented this stew.

1 cup chick-peas, soaked overnight	1 large (28-ounce) can tomatoes, undrained
2 tablespoons oil	2 teaspoons curry powder
2 onions, chopped	¼ teaspoon each ginger, cloves
1 small winter squash, peeled and cut into 1-inch cubes	Dash cayenne
2 to 3 cloves garlic, mashed	Salt

Cover soaked, undrained chick-peas with water, and simmer in a covered saucepan until tender, about 1-1/2 hours. Add water as needed, but try to end up with as much of the water as possible absorbed.

Heat the oil in a large pot or skillet. Sauté onions several minutes over medium heat. Add squash, garlic, tomatoes and seasonings except salt, and bring to a boil. Reduce heat, cover, and simmer 1 hour.

Combine chick-peas and squash mixture. Salt to taste. Simmer together 15 minutes. Serves 8.

Soybeans are a notoriously valuable food, cheap, substantial and containing, among other nutrients, first-rate protein and an abundance of magnesium. I say "notoriously" because we all know about soybeans. Unless they're cooked imaginatively, they taste vile. Some excellent suggestions for using them effectively follow.

Donna's Soyburgers

Donna, her husband and several friends stopped for me on the coast road in California. They were on their way to settle in Oregon, a move they'd dreamed of for years. I camped with them that night in the redwoods along the Navarro River near Mendocino. Donna fried up soyburgers from a huge bowl of this wonderful mixture (chilled, it keeps for days, and solves all your quick-meal problems) and served them on slices of bread with ketchup, cheese, mayonnaise, tomatoes and lettuce.

2 cups soybeans
4¼ cups water
3 to 6 eggs, beaten
½ cup wheat germ
1 stalk celery, finely chopped
2 to 3 cloves garlic, mashed

1 tablespoon poultry seasoning
 (see note)
¼ teaspoon black pepper
1½ teaspoons salt or flavored
 salt (onion, garlic, seasoned)
Oil

First, the soybeans. Donna soaks them overnight, then puts them through the medium blade of her meat grinder. Then she cooks them in 4-1/2 cups water (including the soaking water) for 2 or 3 hours, stirring frequently. This method gives a pleasantly grainy texture. I cook them first (for 4 hours if they're unsoaked, 2 hours if they've been soaked), then put them through the grain mill or meat grinder. This method produces a pastelike texture.

Add the remaining ingredients except oil to the cooked soybean mixture. Form into patties, and fry in oil over medium heat until brown on both sides. Makes 16 medium burgers.

Note: Poultry seasoning gives these soyburgers a meaty flavor. You may improvise a mixture of sage, marjoram, savory and thyme.

Soy Cheeseburgers

Shuffling along the dinner line in the Moon Garden's dirt-floored eight-sided log lodge, I felt painfully like the wrong person in the right place. In the dim light, I could see seven other visitors, most of them college-aged men. Missing from the line were a number of the Oregon family's thirty-five members, discouraged, I gathered, by the number of intruders. And this was *nothing*, several people emphasized; sometimes forty or fifty dinnertime visitors would show up. Several years ago the Moon Garden was featured in a national magazine, and although its location was not revealed, the secret leaked out. Like other communes based on the belief that mankind is a holy family, the Moon Garden family would prefer to include all comers in their circle, but as things stand, they patiently explain to each new arrival that he's welcome to stay one night only. A bearded founding member, long ago a corporate dropout, explained that the need of the visitors for spiritual instruction kept the family from putting its energies into becoming closer. "We have to start at the beginning with each one," he said.

Reaching at last the table where the food had been laid out, I served myself a soy cheeseburger that turned out to be delicious, a piece of atrocious unleavened corn bread and a succulent peach. While I ate, a little blond girl tugged at my sleeve, babbling incomprehensibly. Someone gently explained that she had been born deaf. The child's gaiety and the warmth the family showed her told me all I needed to know about the quality of the Moon Garden's emotional life.

2 cups soybeans	3 tablespoons tamari
4 cups water	¼ teaspoon black pepper
½ cup whole wheat flour	Salt
2 onions, chopped	3 tablespoons oil
2 to 4 cloves garlic, mashed	¼ pound sharp cheese, sliced
¼ cup wheat germ	

I goggled when a woman told me how they'd cooked the soybeans: "We steamed them for three hours in a pressure cooker." "Three hours?" "Right." If you don't have a pressure cooker, cover the soybeans (which will cook faster if they've been soaked overnight; use the soaking liquid as part of the cooking water) with 4 cups water, bring to a boil, cover, reduce heat, and simmer slowly all day and perhaps all the next day, or until very soft, soft enough to mash with a potato masher. Add water when necessary.

Combine mashed soybeans with flour, onions, garlic, wheat germ, black pepper and salt to taste. Heat oil over medium heat, and fry patties until nicely browned. When one side is browned, turn and top with a slice of cheese. Cover the skillet to melt the cheese. Makes 16 medium burgers.

Suzy's Soybean Casserole

While I was staying at Breadloaf in New Mexico (p. 89), the Pride Family arrived in a gaily painted delivery van, with their tepee poles on top. Remnant of a commune in California that had broken up when the owner of the house they occupied raised the rent, the five had crossed and recrossed the country in the last few months. First they had gone up to Atlantis in Oregon and planted the garden that I later admired. Then they headed across the Midwest, stopping over at the Foundlings in Iowa (p. 122) and the farm in Wawa, Minnesota (p.170). By the time I got back to Vermont I was no longer capable of much surprise at learning that Sue, who was visiting my friends there, had lived with the Pride Family in California for seven months. I was glad to be able to tell her that although they had planned to winter in Arizona, Breadloaf's subtle magic had appealed to them, and they had pitched their tepee out behind the pueblo.

The two men displayed quixotic tendencies. Pepe, part Menominee Indian, wore his hair cut like a Mohawk's. The day I left he was busy looking for an old car top from which he meant to make a medallion for the commune's front gate. It would be decorated with a sunburst, and in the center would be a loaf of bread. The women, more practical, took over the kitchen, where they cooked a number of fine meals for the fluctuating but always overlarge population. Those first days put us all in a party mood, and every night some visitor with a little cash would be talked into driving over to the bar on the highway to buy beer for everyone. Later came a purge, but the Pride Family, with their high-energy vibes, were invited to stay.

Kiva had a reputation as an excellent cook. But

somehow I never got a recipe from her, which made it
maddening to be asked first in Iowa, then in Minnesota
and at last in Vermont if she'd given me one. Suzy, on
the other hand, contributed the recipe below. She
dislikes commercially canned foods, which makes me
hesitate to recommend canned corn and tomatoes as
alternatives to the fresh variety. When you live in the
country, where you compost your organic garbage and
burn your trash, "Tin cans just don't go," she says. It
occurred to me that a commune like Breadloaf could
support itself by making miniature geodesic domes out
of sticks and can lids and selling them to tourists, but
no matter.

2 cups cooked soybeans,
  well drained
1½ cups (about 4 ears) corn
  kernels, cooked
2½ cups stewed tomatoes
1 cup (¼-pound) grated sharp
  cheese

½ cup wheat germ
¼ cup stock or bouillon,
  or 2 tablespoons water and
  2 tablespoons tamari
¼ cup snipped parsley
1 teaspoon basil
½ teaspoon thyme

Preheat oven to 350°.

Layer the soybeans, vegetables, cheese and wheat
germ in an oiled baking dish, making two layers of
each. Combine stock and herbs, and pour over. Bake
for 30 minutes. Serves 4.

Baked Soybeans

6 cups beef or vegetable broth
2 cups uncooked soybeans
1 onion, chopped
2 tablespoons tamari
6 ripe tomatoes, sliced, or
  1-pound can tomatoes,
  undrained
1 cup (¼-pound) sharp

cheese, grated, or 1 cup
  cottage cheese
2 onions, halved and sliced
¼ cup molasses or maple
  syrup, or 2 tablespoons
  honey
½ teaspoon salt
¼ teaspoon black pepper

Two days before you want to serve the casserole, prepare the broth, and soak the beans overnight in it. The next day, bring beans and liquid to a boil, reduce heat, and simmer until beans are very tender—about 3 hours. Midway through, add the chopped onion and tamari. Allow beans to sit overnight, to absorb flavors. (This marination may be omitted, but the beans gain greatly in flavor from it.)

Preheat oven to 325°.

Oil a baking dish. Reserve half the cheese, if you are using grated sharp cheese, and one of the sliced tomatoes, or slice a canned tomato. Mix the rest of the cheese and tomatoes and the remaining ingredients with the soybeans and their liquid. (If you are using cottage cheese, mix all of it in.) Turn into the baking dish, and top with the reserved cheese and the tomato. Bake for 1 hour. Serves 8. Excellent reheated the next day.

David Bury, Woolman Hill
School, Massachusetts

Larry's Tofu (Soy Cheese)

Larry, shaggy, affable and easygoing, lives at Om Shanti, in the hills of California's Mendocino County. Once the commune bustled with freaks, but too many visitors impelled most of them to migrate north. Now only four remain behind to occupy the steeply sloping eighteenth-growth forest land, on which seven dwellings stand. These range from an unfinished dome to the Ark, a snakelike structure of bent poles thatched with straw. Larry's home is a tall, narrow little storybook house with gables. It seemed to me that he had very good karma. He survives on food stamps and

government commodities food; the butter is rancid and
the syrup moldy, but he still eats his pancakes with
pleasure. When I returned to San Francisco, he
hitched with me, barefoot. Another girl and I went to a
Chinese restaurant and offered to take him, but he said
no, he was morally opposed to restaurants and would
rather stay outside and guard my friend's guitar. After
our meal we discovered that passing tourists, thinking
his idle, inexpert strumming was a performance, had
given him almost $3—a fortune.

Larry and his friends often go to great lengths over a
meal. The night I stayed there, I didn't feel good, so I
lay upstairs in my sleeping bag all evening. Down
below I could hear music and laughter, and once the
girl I'd come with reported that they were making
knishes. Oh, Lord, I thought enviously, but I just
couldn't get up. The next day, recovered, I asked Larry
how the knishes had been. "Terrible," he answered
cheerfully. The tofu works, however, although it isn't
smooth, like commercial tofu (also known as soy cheese
or bean curd).

First, soak any amount of soybeans overnight. The
next day, put through a grain mill or through the fine
blade of a meat grinder, or run in a blender with
enough of the soaking liquid to permit grinding. Then
add water to the beans until the mixture is the consistency of thin oatmeal. Strain through muslin or
cheesecloth, squeezing out the juice. Grind up the
residue and repeat. With patience, Larry says (he has
plenty of it), you can use it all—I gave up when quite a
bit still remained, but I fed this pulp to the chickens, so
it wasn't wasted. Your result should be a liquid
somewhat thicker than milk.

Pour the "milk" into a heavy pot and carefully heat
just to boiling. Stir often to prevent sticking and

burning, since this will ruin its flavor. A double boiler is the safest way to heat it without burning, but it will take it a long time to come to a boil this way.

When the "milk" is at a boil, you may add, as Larry does, the juice of 1 lemon per every 2 cups "milk" to precipitate curds. (Other recipes recommend letting the "milk" sit in a warm place for a couple of days, until the curds form naturally.) The curd will form a cake with amazing rapidity. Save the remaining liquid for a soup stock. Put the curd, or tofu, in clean muslin or cheesecloth—don't use the cloth you strained the bean mixture through, as it will impart a terrible taste—and squeeze out the water until the tofu is of desired consistency, anything from cottage cheese to cheddar.

Tofu may be served plain, with tamari, or cut into cubes and floated in soup. Larry suggests a whole meal based on tofu. First, marinate the tofu several hours or overnight with some chopped onions and tomatoes, dried Chinese mushrooms and a mixture of 1 part tamari to 4 parts water, to cover. You may use the water left from squeezing the tofu for this.

Then make some Whole Wheat Noodles (p. 33), rolling them out as thin as you can with enough flour to prevent sticking. Cut to any size you want, broad or thin. Bring to a full boil a pot of water left from draining the tofu (if you have any more) and meat or vegetable stock, and add the noodles carefully, so that the water does not stop boiling. Boil 5 minutes. Drain.

In a large skillet or wok, stir-fry a sliced carrot and a couple of stalks of broccoli, cut small, in 2 tablespoons oil. After several minutes, add faster-cooking vegetables such as onions, green beans, mustard greens (especially good), tomatoes, turnips (if you like them crunchy), cabbage, all thinly sliced. Just before the vegetables are done, add the tofu, cut into small cubes, along with everything it's been soaking with. Also add 1 teaspoon cornstarch or arrowroot starch per cup of liquid (approximately) dissolved in a little water or stock. Cook just until liquid thickens, stirring lightly so tofu won't fall to pieces. Serve on top of the noodles, and garnish with some chopped scallions or toasted almonds.

Santa Cruz Susan (p. 140) suggests sautéing tofu, cut into small squares, and sliced mushrooms in peanut or sesame oil over medium-high heat until the tofu is browned and crisp.

Tony's Lentil Loaf

A free use of garlic is one of the characteristics of commune cooking. Garlic is believed to have antibiotic properties, which would tend to explain the widespread ancient custom of wearing a clove of garlic to ward off the evil eye.

2 cups lentils	1 teaspoon each basil, oregano
4 cups water	½ teaspoon each cumin, rose-
2 tablespoons oil	mary, dried dillweed (or 1½
2 onions, chopped	teaspoons fresh snipped dill)
6 cloves garlic, mashed	2 tablespoons snipped parsley
2 stalks celery, chopped	⅛ teaspoon cayenne
2 carrots, grated	¼ pound cheese, cut into
3 eggs, well beaten	hunks (optional)

Bring lentils and water to a boil, reduce heat, and simmer 1 hour. Mash into paste. Heat oil in a skillet, and sauté onions, garlic and celery until soft. Add to lentils, along with other ingredients. Pour into a loaf pan, and top with several spoonfuls of sauce:

2 tablespoons oil	1 tablespoon lemon juice or
1 onion, chopped	vinegar
2 cloves garlic, mashed	1 tablespoon honey
15-ounce can tomato sauce	1/3 cup red wine

Heat oil in a saucepan, and sauté onion and garlic over medium heat. When browned, add tomato sauce, lemon juice or vinegar and honey. Reduce heat, and simmer very slowly for 1 or 2 hours, adding wine gradually.

Bake loaf in a preheated 350° oven for 45 minutes. Serve with remaining sauce. Serves 8.

Tony, Prairie Dog Village, California

Burritos

Herman of the Moon Garden Family in Oregon, balding, bearded, exuberant, a beatnik-turned-hippie, invited me to his plastic-covered dome on what he called Leo Hill. We drank his special garlic and rosehip tonic, and I admired the artifacts on his wall—an elaborate feathered pipe, a God's eye, a wand used in the peyote ceremony. Herman sparkled with enthusiasm about my mission. "I'll write your whole book for you!" he exclaimed. I had come to Oregon too late for the Renaissance Faire in Eugene, a week-long gathering of artists, craftsmen and other folk. Herman and members of his family had sold burritos there. They were so popular, Herman said, that one man came up to him to protest: He'd been trying for three days to buy one before they sold out.

Herman was wickedly delighted when I told him I wasn't a vegetarian. I gathered that he belonged to a coterie of meat eaters within the meat-avoiding but tolerant larger family. The next day I left, to observe the commune's "one night only" rule. Herman urged me to stay. "We're going to roast a whole lamb this afternoon. You could collect the recipe. . . ."

PINTO BEANS:

2 cups pinto beans
4 cups water
3 to 4 cloves garlic
1 onion, chopped
1 bay leaf

3 to 4 green chili peppers,
    chopped (see p. 23)
Salt
Cayenne

Soak beans overnight to shorten cooking time. Combine all ingredients except salt and cayenne, bring to a boil, reduce heat, cover, and simmer several hours, or until soft and creamy. Herman recommends cooking very slowly for 24 hours, but this isn't necessary.

SAUCE:

1 large (28-ounce) can tomatoes
    or 12 ripe tomatoes, chopped
2 to 3 green chili peppers,
    chopped
2 onions, chopped

4 cloves garlic
1 cup (¼-pound) sharp
    cheese, grated
Salt

Combine all ingredients except cheese and salt. Bring to a boil, reduce heat, and simmer 1 or 2 hours, stirring frequently. Add cheese, and stir till it melts. Salt to taste.

2 cups whole wheat flour
¾ teaspoon salt

2 tablespoons oil
2/3 cup warm water

FLOUR TORTILLAS:

Combine flour and salt. Add oil and water, and combine. Knead several minutes. Form into 16 balls. Flatten with a rolling pin, using a little flour to prevent sticking, or in a tortilla press. Heat a griddle over medium heat until quite hot. Bake tortillas very briefly on both sides. If you let them bake until they brown, they will crisp up. Fill as soon as they are done as they are no longer very flexible when they cool.

TO ASSEMBLE:

Have dishes of grated cheese, shredded lettuce and sprouts. Fill each burrito with beans, sauce, cheese, lettuce and sprouts, and roll up. Eat with hands. Serves 8.

Hog Farm Beans and Tortillas

The Hog Farm in New Mexico, famous for its fleet of psychedelically painted buses and its work in feeding the crowds at the Woodstock Festival, has only two rules. One, don't do anything that would hurt anyone else, and two, respect each other's space. Like thousands of visitors to northern New Mexico, I stopped in at the Hog Farm, one of the oldest surviving communes in the country. Trudging two miles up a dusty road in the hot sun, I arrived parched and weary to find a group of young men playing a fast game of basketball. Nearby, a heavyset girl was painting a quotation from *Steppenwolf* on the rear of a bus being readied to take a group to Earth People's Park in Norton, Vermont, for the autumnal equinox festival: "The Magic Theater. Price of admission is your mind."

Inside the A-frame kitchen, two discouraged girls surveyed a collection of dirty dishes, pots and pans. For the next few hours I washed dishes and helped piece a dinner out of the commune's meager supplies. I didn't collect a single recipe.

A week later, at Peter Gray's Valley nearby, I met Vara, who had previously lived at the Hog Farm. She gave me this recipe for what she said was a real Hog Farm specialty. Sometimes the Flow brings you what you want when you least expect it. Beans and Tortillas is actually another recipe for burritos, and you can follow the same procedure as above for preparing the beans and the tortillas. The salsa is what makes this different.

½ cup oil
4 onions, chopped
4 cloves garlic, mashed

2 to 4 green chili peppers,
  chopped (p. 23)
¼ cup cider vinegar

Heat the oil in a skillet. Add onions and garlic, and brown over medium heat. Add chilies and vinegar. Serve hot or cold.

To vary the salsa, add an 8-ounce can tomato sauce. You may omit the green chilies and use instead 1 or 2 tablespoons ground red chili peppers—a seasoning commonly available in New Mexico and California, but unknown in New York or Vermont.

Tortilla Scallop

This free-form recipe adapts well to a large group. First, prepare and bake on a griddle Corn Tortillas (p. 92). Preheat oven to 350°. Lay down a layer of tortillas in a pan. Cover with cooked Pinto Beans (p. 70) and another layer of tortillas. Then put down a layer of thinly sliced zucchini and/or corn kernels, cooked or raw. Sprinkle thickly with grated sharp cheese. Top with another layer of tortillas, then one of green chili peppers, chopped (p. 23). Sprinkle thickly with cheese. Bake for 20 minutes, or until the cheese is melted and the casserole is bubbly.

Lisa, New Mexico

Fruited Stuffed Green Peppers

¾ cup brown rice
2 cups boiling water
8 large green peppers
2 tablespoons oil
2 onions, chopped
2 cloves garlic, mashed
2 tablespoons sunflower seeds
2 tablespoons sesame seeds

¼ cup soy grits
1 tart apple, chopped
2 tablespoons raisins or
  currants
1/3 cup fruit juice (apple,
  grape, apricot nectar, etc.)
3 tablespoons tamari

Cook brown rice in boiling water, or use 1-1/2 cups leftover brown rice. Cut the tops off green peppers, saving the ring of pepper from the top for a salad, and remove the pith. You may leave the seeds in if you wish; as Judith says, "They are a good consistency and I assume are good for you."

In oil, sauté the onions, garlic, sunflower and sesame seeds and soy grits over medium heat until browned. Add the apple, raisins, fruit juice and tamari. Cover skillet, lower heat, and simmer 15 minutes. Preheat oven to 375°.

Combine this mixture with the rice, and fill the peppers with it. Set the peppers in an oiled baking dish, propping them against one another if necessary. Bake for 25 to 30 minutes. The peppers should be tender but firm enough to retain their shapes. Serves 4.

Judith St. Soleil, High Ridge Farm, Oregon

Millet, although a staple grain in Africa and China, is used here chiefly as birdseed. This is a shame, because it contains complete protein and cooks up sweet and fluffy. A professor of nutrition at Columbia University told me that "millet evades digestion easily" unless cooked thoroughly, so I steam it for an hour and a half.

Dorothy's Millet Corn Tamale Pie

1 cup millet
2 tablespoons oil
2 onions, chopped
2 cloves garlic, mashed
2 stalks celery, chopped
1 cup corn kernels, cooked, canned or raw
1 large (15-ounce) can

tomato sauce
2½ cups hot water
2 teaspoons chili powder
⅛ teaspoon cayenne
½ teaspoon salt
¼ pound Cheddar or Jack cheese, grated (1 cup) or sliced

Over medium-high heat, dry-roast millet in a saucepan or skillet until lightly browned. Remove from pan. Add oil to the pan, and brown the onions, garlic and celery over medium heat. When they are soft, add the remaining ingredients except cheese. Lower heat, and steam for 1-1/2 hours, adding water if necessary. At the end, top with the cheese, and steam a few more minutes, or until the cheese melts. Serves 4.

Dulusum Farm, Oregon

Millet Loaf

When I first reached New Mexico, I went to see Tom and Lisa, in the mountains southwest of Taos. I had heard they were good people who often helped orient newcomers to the region. That part of New Mexico is strange. Their village hardly seemed to be in the United States at all; most of the adobe homes had no electricity, and many of the townfolk drew their water from the irrigation ditch that ran down from the high peaks beyond. The Penitentes, a weird Christian sect now outlawed for their self-flagellation, were rumored to meet here in secret. Occasional frightening acts of violence had met the first longhairs to settle the region, but for some time freaks and Chicanos had been coexisting peacefully in their honorable poverty. Mexican cooking, in fact, had become overwhelmingly popular with the newcomers.

Tom and Lisa lived just outside town in the "upper llano" (field). In back of their house was a Japanese bath, an octagonal tub of wood fitted together so tightly that it didn't leak, with a firebox below. I showered first at an outside spigot, then, in water that grew hotter and hotter, soaked away the tension lingering from four days on the road. Tom and another visitor meditated nearby, facing the setting sun and a vista of dozens of miles that fell away into canyons and mountains. Inside, Lisa fixed a simple but complexly flavored vegetable dinner from their irrigated garden. Later Tom, also a cook, gave me the recipe below.

1 cup millet
2 tablespoons butter or oil
2 onions, chopped
4 cloves garlic, mashed
2½ cups water
1 cup milk
½ teaspoon dried dillweed or 1½ teaspoons fresh dill, snipped
¼ teaspoon thyme
¼ teaspoon turmeric or curry powder
¼ cup tamari
¼ teaspoon black pepper
2 stalks celery or Chinese cabbage or beet stalk, chopped
2 tablespoons sesame seeds
2 tablespoons sunflower seeds
1 cup unsalted cashews, coarsely chopped
2 tablespoons sesame or other oil or melted butter

In a skillet over medium-high heat, dry-roast 1/4 cup of the millet. Remove. Heat butter or oil in the skillet, and sauté the onions and garlic.

In a saucepan, bring water and milk to a boil. Slowly add the millet (both browned and unbrowned portions), herbs, turmeric or curry powder, tamari, pepper, and the sautéed onions and garlic. Cover, and simmer 1 hour.

Preheat oven to 350°.

Oil a baking dish. Mix celery, seeds and all but 1/4 cup of the nuts with the millet. Turn into baking dish, and sprinkle the reserved nuts on top. Brush with sesame oil or butter. Bake for half an hour. You may run the casserole under the broiler at the end if you wish, for extra browning. Serves 4.

Potato Thing

2 tablespoons butter or oil
2 onions, sliced into rounds
8 mushrooms, sliced
4 potatoes, boiled and sliced
   in their jackets
4 hard-boiled eggs, sliced
1 small can ripe olives,

chopped
1½ cups half and half,
   evaporated milk or milk
½ cup sour cream
1 teaspoon salt
¼ teaspoon black pepper

Preheat oven to 350°.

Over medium heat, sauté the onions and mushrooms in butter or oil until tender. Combine all ingredients in the skillet or a casserole dish. Bake for 20 minutes. Serve hot or cold. Serves 4.

Communal house in Berkeley

Dorothy's Zucchini

Food is such a popular topic in communal circles that I sometimes gathered recipes without having to ask for them. Potato Thing, above, is one example. I was talking to a friend in a communal house when a young man came up and asked if we were staying for dinner. It was his night to cook, and he was making his favorite recipe, a friend's invention. Dorothy's Zucchini is another. I had dropped by Dulusum Farm in Oregon and was hanging out in the kitchen of one of the houses—the four families at the farm live separately though close together—when a pleasant-faced woman with a Southern drawl entered. "Ah made the best thing for dinner last night!" she exclaimed. "Ah took zucchini . . ."

4 small or 2 medium zucchini,
   thinly sliced (1 ¼ to 1 ½ pounds)
1 onion, chopped
2 cloves garlic, mashed
2 tablespoons water

½ cup wheat germ
2 eggs, beaten
2 tablespoons tamari
Oil

Place zucchini, onion and garlic in a saucepan. Add water. Cover, bring to a boil, reduce heat, and steam 15 minutes over very low heat. Add remaining ingredients except oil and mix.

In a skillet, heat 1/4 inch oil over medium heat. Drop zucchini mixture in by large spoonfuls, and sauté until browned on all sides—a few minutes. Serves 4 as a main dish, 8 as a side dish.

Vegetable Pizza

I was offered quite a few recipes for vegetable pizza—including a macrobiotic version without tomatoes or cheese that featured instead winter squash, carrots and parsnips—but I think Lou's is the best. He's a sunny, radiant idealist whom I met while

he was working in the kitchen of a home for delinquent
boys in New Hampshire (p. 158).

5 tablespoons oil
1 medium zucchini or summer
   squash, sliced
1 large carrot, sliced
1 onion, sliced
1 small can tomato paste
Salt and pepper

2 green peppers, chopped
¼ pound mushrooms, sliced
Pizza crust (below)
1 teaspoon oregano
1 cup (¼-pound) grated
   sharp cheese

Heat 3 tablespoons of the oil in a skillet, and slowly
sauté zucchini, carrot and onions over medium heat for
10 minutes. Add tomato paste, lower heat, cover, and
steam 15 minutes. Remove from skillet, and add salt
and pepper to taste.

In skillet, heat remaining oil over medium heat.
Sauté green peppers and mushrooms until soft.

For the crust, follow the recipe below, or use part of
any whole grain bread dough, rolled out, or crust for a
double-crust pie. Preheat oven to 425° and bake crust
for 5 minutes.

Spread crust with the zucchini mixture; then
sprinkle with peppers and mushrooms. Sprinkle
oregano over that, and top with the cheese. Bake at
425° for 15 minutes. (Other good additions: chopped
green chili peppers, tuna fish, sardines, ripe olives.)

PIZZA CRUST:

1 package yeast
1 cup warm water
1 teaspoon honey

2 1/3 cups whole wheat flour
1 teaspoon salt

Sprinkle yeast into warm water. Add the honey. Allow to stand 5 minutes. Mix flour and salt, and add. Knead several minutes on an oiled board to avoid adding any more flour. Oil your hands as well so the dough won't stick to them. Let rise until doubled in a covered bowl. Knead again briefly, roll out, and use at once with no further rising.

III. Meat
(and One Fish)

If you limited your traveling to the West Coast, you'd probably come away with the impression that meat plays little part in the commune diet. I left California with only a handful of meat recipes. In New Mexico and later New England, however, I was surprised to find vegetarianism more the exception than the rule. At least half the communes I visited in these areas were fattening pigs and offed their surplus roosters with alacrity. Fitting that Crow Farm in Oregon should raise beef cattle, since legend among the pacifistic freaks of the Willamette Valley attributes Crow's notorious virile aggressiveness to their meat-eating ways; but to find steer at a quiet commune in Vermont (p. 45)! New Mexico communes celebrate with ground beef whenever they can and even hold wiener roasts (p. 191). High Ridge Farm once came close to a split over the question of whether or not to eat their billies—

while Marjory at Sunflower Farm in Ontario (p. 130) praised with gleaming eyes the deliciousness of goat meat. The Dreamers in Vermont had just butchered a hog when I arrived and planned to kill another the next day; their sister commune Evenstar in Oregon would never think of raising meat. At the Black Flag in New Hampshire I saw a photograph of their ram Frank, head cocked, soft eyes gazing wistfully at the camera. It was a shock to learn he'd since been eaten.

Why this geographical difference? A popular explanation on both coasts is that the rigors of winter in New England and the high country of the Southwest make meat eating necessary for energy. I myself suspect the reason has more to do with spiritual climate. Commune people in California and Oregon seemed more religious and idealistic, less intellectual, political and profane than their counterparts elsewhere. Country freaks, you'll find, are characteristically gentle and tolerant, but the West Coast has a special quality of intuitive spirituality. Does this come back to the easygoing weather? Or is it because West Coast people have access to so many fine psychedelics? I don't know. At any rate, even meat-eating communes usually have a few vegetarian members, and vice versa. It's typical that these loosely structured groups should encompass such different philosophies and settle the problem simply by having two spaghetti sauces—one with meat and one without (p. 86)!

I'd always assumed that a moral objection to killing was the basis for vegetarianism. Far from it. Some people I talked to abstained from meat because American livestock are fattened artificially with injections of hormones. Others believed that meat is inherently adulterated, by the adrenalin that courses through the animal's body at death and by uric wastes in the tissues. Another argument claimed that man, like other apes, is by nature a fruitarian, who learned to eat meat accidentally during the Ice Age but whose digestive system is unable to cope with it.*

The most widespread motive for a meatless diet is economic. Many practicing vegetarians will eat meat with delight when the opportunity arises—for example, when their parents visit the commune in Bermuda shorts and bouffants (a common summer occurrence) and take them away to the local Holiday Inn for a steak. Some are seasonal vegetarians, like Michele of Hobbiton, on a little island off Vancouver, who told me, "It's necessary to eat meat in the winter, but not in the summer. I can't feel spiritual when I eat meat. It drags me down to a lower level." The attitude that appealed to me most of all was voiced by a thin, lightly garbed man at Wheeler's Ranch in California. "I take the Zen position," he said. "If someone prepares food for you, eat it."

Chili con Carne

The Furry Freak Brothers of New Mexico, who take their name from the slovenly, dope-smoking folk heroes of Zap Comics, made me part of their family, and I will enjoy the memory forever. I arrived without a flashlight and on foot one moonless night. The sound of rock music in the darkness drew me off the rutted road up their mesa. Stumbling recklessly up a stony hillside, then through a pine woods, I finally glimpsed a light. The music was pouring from a little gabled house set among the trees. By it stood a young woman who had stepped outside for a breath of night air. She watched

*For a good discussion of the pros and cons of meat, see *Natural Life Styles II* (Box 150, New Paltz), pp. 29-31.

unperturbed as I lurched out of the dark, an unlikely apparition-with-backpack. "Hello," she greeted me with a smile. "I'm Sunny."

Inside, most of the family of fourteen lay sprawled about on couches and rugs in comfortable, winey intimacy. A similar party occurred spontaneously every night of my five-day stay, although I was repeatedly told that "we never do this." The community consists of numerous small houses scattered well apart among the pines. Most members come from Texas, and Texas longhairs, despite the persecution they endure in their home state, are the friendliest, most relaxed people I've met anywhere. Although they don't consider themselves a commune (few do), they cook and eat in a central kitchen, raise chickens and pigs communally, and joyfully relish their good times together. Occasionally in my later weeks in Taos, seeing the Freak Brothers' van speed by emblazoned with a spectacular rendition of their namesakes, I would feel a pang for the closeness I'd briefly been part of.

One of the men gave me this recipe, originally orchestrated for twenty. It involves several pots and pans, but what a chili!

1 recipe Pinto Beans (p. 70)	1 teaspoon oregano
2 tablespoons oil	2 teaspoon ground red chili
3 onions, chopped	peppers (see note)
4 cloves garlic, mashed	1 teaspoon cumin (see note)
2 green peppers, chopped	2 green chili peppers,
1 pound ground chuck, crumbled	chopped (p. 23)
¼ pound bacon, chopped	2 tablespoons snipped parsley
1 large (28-ounche) can	½ teaspoon salt
tomatoes, undrained	

Prepare Pinto Beans, using 2 cups beans.

In a large skillet, heat oil over medium heat, and sauté onions, garlic, green peppers and chuck until

lightly browned. Pour off any fat that accumula
Fry bacon until crisp.

In a saucepan, simmer tomatoes and seasonings
while you prepare everything else.

Combine all ingredients in a kettle. Simmer together
over low heat for 2 hours or more, adding water if it
becomes too dry. Serves 8. Good with rice. Like all
stews, chili is even better the next day.

Note: If you can't obtain ground red chili peppers,
substitute 1 tablespoon chili powder for it and the
cumin. This fiery-red but mild seasoning is invariably
used, along with cumin and oregano, instead of chili
powder in New Mexico.

Tamale Pie

A colorful reputation preceded me to the Tribe in the
mountains of southern Colorado. The week before,
hitching from a small town in New Mexico to
Breadloaf, I'd been given a lift by two young men from
the Tribe. They were returning from an Indian festival
in Arizona. "Do you have any grass?" they asked me.
As it happened, a friend had just given me a little
homegrown—the only time on my trip that I carried
any dope—and we all got high. The next week, on my
way to Denver to start East, I persuaded the fellow who
was giving me and three other hitchhikers a ride to
drop in at the Tribe, a mere twenty or thirty miles out
of our way, straight up. We arrived, with several
bottles of wine bought on the long-haired driver's
expense account, just at suppertime. The two boys I
knew saw me coming and shouted, "That's the girl with
the far-out dope! Hey, juicy Lucy, how's your cook-

book?'' Of course, I didn't have any grass left, which tended to diminish my image.

Although it was only September, a heavy snow had already fallen, but the spirited family of thirty-five, which had gotten together that spring, was sticking to its plan of wintering in tepees; only one permanent structure had been completed. Despite the raw wind, dinner—spaghetti with two sauces, one with meat and one without—had been prepared in an outdoor kitchen and was eaten at an unsheltered table. I thought they were crazy. The commune's energy flow is intricately linked with its rock band, which performs one night a week in a cafe twenty miles away. This recipe was contributed by the band's equipment manager, who had formerly worked for top San Francisco groups like the Grateful Dead and the Jefferson Airplane.

2 tablespoons oil
1 pound ground chuck, crumbled
1 onion, chopped
2 green chili peppers, chopped (p. 23)
1-pound can corn, drained, or corn from 4 ears, cooked or raw
1 cup canned tomatoes, undrained, or 4 ripe tomatoes, quartered
1 small can tomato paste
1 square unsweetened baking chocolate or 1 tablespoon carob powder
1 tablespoon molasses
1 rounded tablespoon peanut butter
¼ teaspoon cinnamon
¼ teaspoon cloves
2 tablespoons sesame seeds

Preheat oven to 350°.

Heat oil in a skillet over medium-high heat, and sauté the chuck and onion for several minutes. Add remaining ingredients, lower heat, and simmer together until chocolate and peanut butter melt.

Prepare Crust (opposite), and roll out. Oil a pie plate or baking dish. In the bottom, put half the crust. Pour in filling, and top with the other half of the crust. Bake for 30 minutes. Serves 6 to 8.

CRUST:

1 ½ cups cornmeal, preferably masa harina	½ teaspoon salt ½ cup oil

Combine all ingredients. Masa harina, cornmeal treated with lime, is the kind of cornmeal used in Mexican cooking for corn tortillas. It can be obtained in areas where there is a Mexican community. If you can't get it, use regular cornmeal. The result will still be delicious, but the crust will not hold together. Pat it instead of rolling it.

Lasagna

Why has almost every recipe in this chapter been contributed by a man? This immensely tasty version of lasagna—the secret lies in the combination of cheeses—is the invention of Tony, of Prairie Dog Village in California.

CHEESE SAUCE:

2 onions, chopped
2 cloves garlic, mashed
2 tablespoons oil
1 pound ground chuck and 1 pound ground pork, crumbled, or 2 pounds ground chuck, crumbled
1 pound Italian sausage, sliced
1 small can tomato paste
1 small (8-ounce) can tomato

sauce
1 large (28-ounce) can tomatoes
1 teaspoon each basil, rosemary, oregano
¼ cup snipped parsley
Sherry (optional)
¼ pound mushrooms, sliced and sauteed in 2 tablespoons oil or butter (optional)

In a large skillet or kettle, sauté the onions and garlic in the oil over medium-high heat, until browned. Add crumbled meats and sliced sausage, and brown, pouring off fat as it accumulates. Add all remaining ingredients except sherry and mushrooms. Stir well, lower heat, and simmer 1 to 4 hours (adding water if necessary). Near the end, add a dash of sherry and the mushrooms if desired.

CHEESE LAYER:

2 cups ricotta or small-curd cottage cheese
1 cup Parmesan cheese
2 cups grated Cheddar cheese
2 cups sour cream
2 eggs, beaten

Combine.

NOODLES:

Cook 16 ounces broad noodles (see note) until slightly underdone. Drain, rinse, and drain again.

SPINACH:

Wash 1 pound spinach (a bucketful). Put it in a tightly covered heavy saucepan with the water that clings to its leaves and place over medium-low heat. Steam 4 or 5 minutes, or until wilted.

TO ASSEMBLE:

Preheat oven to 375°. Oil a large casserole dish (a roasting pan is the right size). In it, place half the noodles. Cover with half the spinach and its juices, then half the cheese mixture and half the sauce. Repeat. Top with a good sprinkling of Parmesan or cheddar. Bake for 30 minutes. Serves 12.

Note: Neither Italian sausage nor lasagna noodles qualify as natural ingredients. For the latter, you may substitute large noodles prepared according to the recipe on p. 0, cooked in boiling water. Or convert the lasagna to an Italian moussaka: Slice a large eggplant in quarter-inch slices, oil and lightly salt them, and bake or broil them at moderate heat until tender. Use between layers instead of noodles.

Torgerson's Mexican-Italian Blintzes

I spent an hour of my afternoon at Crow Farm in

Oregon watching runaway pigs being chased back into their pens. Later, in the kitchen, I looked curiously at the snack Torgerson had concocted for himself and his lady. "Give her some," he ordered, and she gave me some.

SAUCE:

1 cup ketchup or 1 small can tomato paste and 1 tablespoon honey
1 cup water

1 small onion, chopped
⅛ teaspoon cayenne
¼ teaspoon thyme
¼ teaspoon basil

BLINTZES:

1 recipe Swedish Pancakes omitting the vanilla
¼ teaspoon crushed red pepper
1 pound ground chuck
½ teaspoon fennel seeds

1 tablespoon oil
½ cup cottage cheese
½ cup mozzarella, Jack or Colby cheese, grated
Parmesan cheese (optional)

Mix together sauce ingredients, and simmer.

Meanwhile, prepare 8 Swedish pancakes in a small skillet. Save the rest of the batter for breakfast.

Knead the fennel seeds and red pepper into the chuck. Heat oil in a skillet over medium heat, and crumble in the meat. Brown.

Combine the meat with the cottage cheese. Preheat oven to 400°.

Fill each pancake with a big spoonful of the meat-cheese mixture. Top with a spoonful of the sauce, mozzarella cheese and a good shake of Parmesan cheese, if you have it. Bake for 10 minutes. Serve with the rest of the sauce. Serves 4.

Chuck's Chicken Tacos

Breadloaf was the only commune I wrote ahead to. I had heard such terrible stories about the visitor problem at the famous New Mexico commune that I wanted to be sure I arrived at the right time. Amazingly, I got an answer back. It read:

DEAR LUCY,
 First of all, please do visit! Don't spread it around, but every person on the face of the earth is welcome to visit here. Sometimes it gets crowded, sometimes lonely.
 By saying you're after commune recipes, do you mean you're starting one? I wish to encourage you with the thot that *anything* along that line is possible—depending on four factors: the individuals, the property, the physical arrangement, the social arrangment. Frinstance: group marriage of 24 in dome in mountains, self-sufficient— or—loosely affiliated couples cooperatively farming with outside gigs and houses hidden from each other, etc. (Excerpt from my rap to University of New Mexico Free University.)
 I, Douglas no. 1, have been living here two years and will be gone by the time you come by, which is too bad cuz I'm looking for people interested in starting *something*, *somewhere*. C'est la vie.
 Love and encouragement, peace, etc.
                                              DOUGLAS M.

The young man who drove me from Lama to Breadloaf said, "You'll sure be welcome there. One night this summer, unbeknownst to anyone, all the chicks split." Breadloaf periodically loses its population and gains a new one. At this point five men and one woman lived there, and she had just arrived the week before. ("God brought me, much to my surprise," she replied when I asked her why she'd happened to come.) Breadloaf's main building is an adobe pueblo with twelve private rooms, a kitchen and a sunken communal room called the Circle. Several rooms in the pueblo, built four years ago by poets, artists and idealists, stood empty. I stayed in the Pit House, an underground chamber like a kiva some distance away which you entered down a narrow stairway dug between walls of dense sand.

The next day a Labor Day weekend deluge of visitors began. They came on motorcycles, in vans, old Ramblers, school buses, some passing through, some hoping to stay for the winter. When the permanent residents could no longer bear the sociable chaos, they got together and kicked out most of the newcomers, explaining to each one that the arid, irrigated land could support only a limited number of people. Those invited to remain included the Pride Family (p. 63), a sultry divorcee who blew in from Chicago with her three young sons and announced she was staying, and an introverted dropout from a seminary. Again Breadloaf was going through its cycle.

Chuck, tall and soft-spoken, had lived through two years of Breadloaf's transfusions. He and several of the other men belonged to the Southwest Fire-fighters Association. The previous summer they had earned $800 each fighting forest fires in Arizona, but since this had been a poor year for fires, Chuck got up early every morning and went to work building a house in a nearby village. He was of Mexican ancestry and an excellent cook. "Do you want my recipe for chili sauce?" he'd ask unexpectedly. Or, "You want that recipe for chicken tacos?"

About 4-pound stewing chicken	1 teaspoon salt
2 tablespoons oil	12 Corn Tortillas (p. 92)
2 onions, chopped	Guacamole II (p.147)
1 green pepper, chopped	Grated sharp cheese
1½ teaspoons cumin	Shredded lettuce
¼ teaspoon cayenne	

"Take an old rooster out to the woodpile . . ." Chuck began. Cover the chicken with water, bring to a boil, cover, lower heat and simmer for 1 hour, or until chicken is tender. Remove from broth and cool. Then take the meat, and chop it from the bones. (Return the bones and skin to the broth, add the giblets, and simmer an hour or two with an onion and a stalk of celery to make a chicken soup, which you won't use in this recipe.)

Heat oil in a large skillet over medium heat. Brown onions, green pepper and chicken meat until the onion is soft. Add cumin, cayenne and salt.

Prepare Corn Tortillas (below). To assemble tacos, fill first with the chicken mixture, then the Guacamole, next the cheese and lettuce. Serves 4 to 6. We couldn't locate an avocado, so we had this once with Chili Sauce Piquante (p. 157), once with Quick Hot Sauce, doubled (p. 107).

CORN TORTILLAS:

As I've noted, authenic Mexican corn tortillas are made with masa harina, a form of cornmeal treated with lime. Regular cornmeal by itself will not hold together. Here in Vermont, I make corn tortillas very successfully by this recipe: Combine 1 cup whole wheat flour, 1 cup cornmeal, 3/4 teaspoon salt, 2 tablespoons oil and 2/3 cup warm water. Knead several minutes. You can just squeeze the dough in your hands instead of kneading it on a board. Then divide the dough into 12 balls. Roll each one out in a circle, sprinkling the rolling surface liberally with additional cornmeal. Pat the first ball of dough on the cornmeal; then turn it over, so that the rolling pin won't stick. (Or use a tortilla press.)

For tacos, roll the tortillas out thin. Heat 1/4 inch oil (see p. 24) in a skillet until very hot. Fry tortillas one at a time for 35 to 40 seconds, pressing down the centers if they puff up. Lift them out with a turner, and fold in

half as you do so. Drain on paper towels or newspaper
(they won't pick up the print). If you cook them any
longer or delay about folding them, they will get too
crisp to fold.

Three Rooster Recipes

I met many men and women in country places who
were intimate with nature. My friend Mary in Vermont
is one of them. Mud, blood, shit, natural violence—
nothing in nature threatens her. Consequently, she's
able to be closer to her children than most women. Her
compost pile gives her the satisfaction of an artistic
creation. Her gardens prosper. She predicts the
weather. She faces down disasters. The other day I
killed the yeast in a batch of bread with water that was
too hot. Mary dissolved more yeast, oiled her huge
salad bowl, propped it on a chair, and sat in a chair
facing it. With the bowl between her knees, she
kneaded in the new yeast, throwing herself tirelessly
against the dough. The bread rose. Mary enjoys rhyth-
mic, strenuous work and any task that takes her into
the woods. Lugging water from the spring is a chore for
me, but she enjoys it: She sees stories in the tracks she
notices in the snow and finds pleasure in listening to
silence: She talks to her chickens with affection, but
when she decides to have chicken for dinner, she offs
the rooster herself. She's found that if she skins and
bones the chicken before cooking it, then dices the
meat, it goes farther. Soup is then made from the
bones, skin, giblets and feet. Three recipes for boned
raw chicken meat follow. The first was invented by
Mary, the other two by me.

I. TAMARI CHICKBITS

Meat of ½ chicken
2 tablespoons oil
1/3 cup water
2 tablespoons tamari
1 tablespoon arrowroot starch
  or cornstarch

1½ cups chicken broth
1 to 2 cloves garlic, crushed
1/3 cup wine or beer
1 teaspoon honey
Salt and pepper
Cooked brown rice or bulgur

Cut meat into small cubes or strips. Brown in oil. Add water and tamari. Cover, and simmer until the chicken is tender—20 or 25 minutes.

Dissolve starch in broth, and add to chicken along with the garlic, wine or beer and honey. Simmer, uncovered, stirring, until mixture thickens and boils. Season to taste with salt and pepper. Serve with brown rice or bulgur. Serves 4.

II. CHICKEN WITH APPLES

Meat of ½ chicken
2 tablespoons oil or butter
4 tart apples, sliced
½ cup wine or beer

1 tablespoon honey chicken
Salt and pepper
Cooked brown rice
  or bulgur

Sauté chicken in oil as above. After several minutes, add apples, and sauté several more minutes. Pour in wine or beer and honey. Cover, reduce heat, and simmer 25 minutes. Salt and pepper to taste. Serve with brown rice or bulgur. Serves 4.

III. CHICKEN IN PEANUT SAUCE

Meat of ½ chicken
2 tablespoons oil
2 onions, chopped
6 ripe tomatoes, cut into
  quarters, or 1-pound can of
  tomatoes, undrained

1/3 cup peanut butter
2 tablespoons tamari
1 red or green chili pepper,
  finely chopped (p. 23)
2 cloves garlic, crushed
Cooked brown rice or bulgur

Sauté chicken in oil as above. After several minutes, add onions, and sauté until tender. Add tomatoes, cover, lower heat, and simmer half an hour. Stir in the remaining ingredients. Simmer several minutes; then serve on brown rice or bulgur. Serves 4.

Chicken Livers in Wine

Vermont was deep in golden leaves when I went to see the Dreamers. Up the lane past the point where cars could go, my ankles sank in leaves. Golden leaves drifted down around us as the family and I talked outside their square little house. On an outdoor wood stove, the fat of a pig slaughtered the day before was being rendered into lard. Peter stood stirring it. "Is it going to melt down?" he asked doubtfully, staring at the hunks of fat. I'd made soap from suet the winter before and had the same doubts. "It will," I reassured him.

The family had recently undergone a split, with half leaving to start their own community. The nine remaining were breathlessly young boys and girls and one much-cuddled baby. They'd built their house two autumns before, racing the coming of the snow cover. The townspeople, shaking their heads, called them "a bunch of dreamers." This autumn their harvest bulged the root cellar and spilled up into the main room, where I gaped at their watermelon-sized hubbard squashes. On a wall I noticed a photograph of their good friends, the Evenstar Family in Oregon.

Several Dreamers clustered around me to offer recipes. As I scribbled in the ecstasy of acquisition, their soft voices caressed and soothed me exquisitely.

This dish, which they say they've made there, must at most times be a dream to them indeed—chicken livers, butter, red wine. . . .

Salt and pepper
1 pound chicken livers
(see note)
Whole wheat flour

2 tablespoons butter
1 tablespoon oil
Red wine
Cooked brown rice or bulgur

Salt and pepper the chicken livers and roll them in flour. Heat butter and oil in a thick frying pan over medium heat until the foam on the butter subsides (a trick Peter learned from Julia Child). Add livers, and sauté, turning constantly with a spoon, until just browned. Add wine to a depth of 1/4 inch. Reduce heat, and simmer until the wine and flour form a sauce. Test the livers and see if they're done to your liking. If not, add a little more red wine, and simmer longer. Serve with brown rice or bulgur. Serves 4.

Note: You may use any type of liver, cubed.

Goat Stew

Dairy goats are one of the two most popular commune animals, chickens being the other. Vegetarian communes have little use for their male kids, but Marjory of Sunflower Farm in Ontario (p. 130) urges goat raisers to eat them. Goat, which she sampled in Jamaica, is her favorite of all meats. Adult billies have scent glands on the inside of the hind leg by the joint which must be cut out immediately after slaughtering, but kids under the age of six months lack this gland and are far more tender. Like rabbit, goat is lean and takes better to stewing than roasting or broiling. If you do roast the leg, Marjory says, roast it slowly.

Cut goat meat into cubes. Heat several tablespoons of oil in a kettle, and brown several chopped onions and mashed cloves of garlic over medium heat. Add meat, and brown. Cover with water, bring to a boil, add a bay leaf, lower heat, and simmer 2 hours. Forty-five minutes before you want to serve it, add several sliced carrots and diced potatoes to the pot. At the end, salt and pepper to taste.

Fish Almondine

I have remarked that the Furry Freak Brothers of New Mexico was the most pleasure-oriented, libertine commune I visited. This is one of their more voluptuous recipes.

Oil a baking pan that will fit under the broiler. Lay any kind of fish fillets in it. Dot generously with butter, and sprinkle with basil. Cook under a hot broiler for several minutes, or until browned. Do not turn, and do not overcook; fish cooks very quickly.

Meanwhile, brown 1/2 cup (1 stick) butter in a saucepan or small skillet over medium heat. Add 1/2 cup slivered almonds, and brown them. At the last minute, squeeze in the juice of 1 lemon. Pour over the fish. Serve at once.

IV. Eggs

Chickens crop up on communes everywhere. We have sixteen Comet chickens. All we have to do is feed and water them (they drink a lot of water) and count our eggs—eight to twelve a day from fourteen hens. When they first started laying in the fall, we lost eggs because we couldn't keep them from flying the coop and nesting outside. At Sunflower Farm in Ontario, the coop yard is covered with a web of strings to prevent this. Fortunately, our hens were afraid of the snow at first. Having been kept in their yard by it, they got into the habit of laying in their nesting boxes. Now, although they run freely even on the coldest days, egg yield remains steady.

A well-designed coop, which I saw at High Ridge Farm, has hinged boards on the outside that are lifted up to give unobtrusive access to the laying boxes in-

side. (In good weather there, many of the chickens fly
up in the trees near the coop to roost at night—a
startling sight.) By far the most original coop I saw, at
Elfhome in New Hampshire, had a yard enclosed by a
structure of bent cedar poles covered with chicken
wire. Swinging mobiles were provided for the chickens
to roost on.

In the field of sincere chicken lovers, Larry of Om
Shanti in California carried off all honors. He had a
flock of ten hens, but only one, which had spontaneously started nesting in the kitchen next to the
sink, ever gave him an egg. The rest deposited theirs in
the woods. I asked him why he bothered to keep the
deadbeats. "I like them," he answered. "They're
pretty."

Eggs Woodstock

This magnificent recipe comes from one of my very
first communes, the True Light Beavers of Woodstock,
New York (p. 148). They took their name from some T-
shirts which a member had found in a city thrift shop.
Once in the city a young man approached a Beaver
who was wearing one and exclaimed, "Where did you
get that shirt? That's the name of our Zen temple
basketball team!"

2 tablespoons butter or oil
2 onions, sliced into rounds
¼ pound mushrooms, sliced
1 cup sour cream
4 eggs
1 tablespoon fresh snipped dill

or 1 teaspoon dried dill-
   weed
½ teaspoon paprika
½ teaspoon salt
⅛ teaspoon black pepper
¼ pound Cheddar cheese,
   sliced

Sauté onions in butter or oil in a saucepan for 5 minutes over medium heat. Add mushrooms, and sauté another 5 minutes. Add sour cream, and lower heat. Simmer 5 minutes.

Make four depressions in the sour cream with a spoon. Break the eggs into them. Do not stir; the eggs should sit on top of the sour cream. Sprinkle with seasonings. Cover, and steam five minutes.

Top with slices of cheese and run under a hot broiler for 2 minutes, or cover and steam until the cheese melts. Serves 4.

Vegetable Omelet

Jackie, the beautiful black dancer who gave me this recipe at the Brush Brook Family in Oregon, had just returned from teaching a dance class at a free school in a nearby town.

3 tablespoons oil
1 onion, chopped
2 cups chopped vegetables
  (see note)
6 eggs
¼ teaspoon basil
¼ teaspoon thyme
¼ teaspoon tarragon

Pinch savory
2 cloves garlic, mashed
1 teaspoon Worcestershire
  or tamari
½ teaspoon salt
¼ pound cheese—Cheddar,
  Jack, mozzarella, etc.

Heat oil in skillet. Stir-fry onion and vegetables until tender over medium heat. Beat eggs with seasonings, garlic and salt. Pour over vegetables. Top with slices of cheese. Cover, and cook for 8 minutes over medium heat, or until eggs are cooked to your liking. Do not flip. The omelet will get brown and crusty on the bottom. Serves 4.

Note: Use one vegetable or a mixture. Good ones include broccoli, cabbage, cauliflower, celery, green pepper, mushrooms.

While I was typing this in Vermont, a homesteading neighbor dropped in and looked over my shoulder. "I used to go with a beautiful black dancer named Jackie," he said in surprise, "and last I heard, she was living in a commune in Oregon!"

Vegetable Eggs

A phenomenal recipe.

In a wok or skillet, roast a handful of seeds—sesame, sunflower, buckwheat, pumpkin—over high heat until browned, stirring often. Set aside. Add oil to pan, and stir-fry a couple of onions, chopped, and two or three mashed cloves of garlic. After a few minutes, add a pile of vegetables—chopped spinach or cabbage, shredded beet or kohlrabi, to name a few possibilities—and stir-fry for a couple of minutes. Break several eggs on top of the vegetables, and sprinkle with grated sharp cheese. Cover, and steam 10 minutes over medium heat, or until done to your liking. Sprinkle with the roasted seeds.

You may also top the eggs with several spoonfuls of tahini (p. 59) before adding cheese.

Michele, Hobbiton, B.C.

Omelet Outrageous

This recipe, from Doug of the Furry Freak Brothers in New Mexico, was originally given for twenty and called for two dozen eggs. I've reluctantly scaled it down. They do everything so lavishly.

6 eggs
1 cup cottage cheese
½ teaspoon basil
½ teaspoon oregano
½ teaspoon salt
¼ teaspoon black pepper
¼ pound mushrooms, sliced
2 tablespoons butter or oil
1 cup sprouts, preferably

alfalfa
¼ cup chopped cashews or
  other nuts
½ cup grated Cheddar
  cheese
1 tablespoon sesame seeds
1 tablespoon sunflower
  seeds
Sour cream or yogurt

Preheat oven to 350°.

Beat together eggs, cottage cheese and seasonings until foamy, using a whisk or beater. Oil a baking dish. Pour in mixture, and bake until omelet is semisolid— thickened but still runny.

Meanwhile, sauté mushrooms in butter or oil. Stir the mushrooms into the semicooked eggs. Sprinkle sprouts on top of the eggs, sprinkle the nuts on top of the sprouts, and return to the oven for a few more minutes. Remove from the oven, sprinkle with grated cheese and, last of all, with the seeds. Put back in the oven until the cheese melts and the seeds are browned. Serve with sour cream or yogurt. Serves 4.

Huevos Rancheros

I stepped off the midday ferry to Vancouver Island with the addresses of two communities. They'd been given to me by a sympathetic couple at Rainbow City Hall in Vancouver, where British Columbia's own remarkable *Whole Earth Catalog* (*the B.C. Access Catalog*) is published. Both names looked enticing, but one, a group of three families who kept bees for a living, particularly intrigued me.

With some difficulty, I found my way there. Nobody was home. While I waited for the beekeepers to return,

I looked around the property, on which stood three large A-frames. Cautiously I peeped inside one. The interior was charming, but a modern kitchen contained cake mixes, plastic cereal—shelf after shelf of junk food. The other kitchens were similarly stocked, and the houses gave off strong single-family vibes. Being found here suddenly seemed embarrassingly inappropriate. I shouldered my pack and hurried out to the highway, figuring I'd try my other possibility, the Galaxy Light Movers forty miles up the coast.

Now my luck turned: Gary, another hitchhiker, invited me home to meet his wife, Marilyn, a fine organic cook, and stay overnight. I accepted with relief. Then a pickup truck pulled up for us, driven by a bearded longhair. In the back sat a bone-tired Danish girl and a Japanese man. Gary, with a sudden flash, asked if they were from the Galaxy Light Movers. They were, they replied wearily. In fact, they were just returning from one of the construction-and-maintenance jobs by which the commune supported itself. With a single word my faith in the Flow had been restored. Delightedly, I told them I'd be over tomorrow.

Marilyn was in the garden with the couple's apricot baby, Alexandra. Their house was on the highway behind a hamburger stand, repulsive to the couple, dedicated vegetarians. Low-rock music blared from a loudspeaker in front. When we went inside, Gary put on a Jethro Tull album to drown it out. He offered me some homegrown grass, saying with characteristic intensity, "Don't take it if you aren't going to smoke it. Lots of women don't really like to get high, and they just sit there and pretend to smoke." Then he made me some of his special herbal tea. He was so deeply interested in herbal healing that he had recently enrolled in a correspondence course in naturepathy. The tea contained "alfalfa for vitamins A, B12, E, K, and niacin, dulse for B1, B2, B12, E and iodine, saffron for B2, comfrey for its general healing powers, licorice root for hormones and phosphorus, and Hydrocotyle asiatica (fo-ti-tieng) for vitamin X, which enables you to live 200 years, as well as vitamin C, iron, and magnesium."

Marilyn and Gary met in Mexico, where this recipe originates.

For each serving, roll out a large Corn Tortilla (p. 92), and fry it on both sides on a griddle or in a skillet in a little oil until brown. Fry an egg or two, and put it on the tortilla. Top with a slice of cheese—Cheddar, Jack, Gouda—and then with some slices of onion and green pepper. Last, pour over a large spoonful of Quick Hot Sauce (below). Bake in a hot oven a few minutes to melt the cheese, or serve at once.

QUICK HOT SAUCE

1 small can tomato paste
1 can water
1 to 2 cloves garlic
1 tablespoon vinegar

1 tablespoon honey (optional)
1 chili pepper, chopped (p.23),
    or ¼ teaspoon cayenne

Combine all ingredients, and simmer together for 10 minutes to half an hour, adding water if it becomes too dry.

Marilyn, Vancouver Island

Egg and Mushroom Pie

An English recipe from an English lady.

Crust for a single-crust pie
½ pound mushrooms, chopped
  small
2 cloves garlic, mashed
¼ teaspoon thyme
¼ teaspoon rosemary

2 tablespoons oil or butter
6 eggs
2 tablespoons milk
¼ teaspoon salt
⅛ teaspoon black pepper

Prepare a single piecrust. Bake (see p. 24) 5 minutes at 400° to harden. Meanwhile, sauté the mushrooms, garlic and herbs in oil or butter over medium heat until the mushrooms are browned. Beat the eggs, milk, salt and pepper until foamy. Combine with the mushroom mixture, and pour into pie shell. Bake at 400° for 20 minutes, or until the filling rises like an omelet. The filling will only partially fill the shell when you pour it in, but when it rises, it will come up to the rim. Serves 6.

Carleen, Prairie Dog Village, California

V. Grains
and Legumes

While properly cooked vegetables are rich in natural flavor, grains—the other mainstay of the commune diet—need seasoning with generous dashes of imagination to save them from dreariness. These grain and bean recipes demonstrate the special cleverness of the commune cook. Another resourceful gambit is to serve grains in pairs. Wheat berries, bulgur wheat and especially millet and soybeans contain complete high-quality protein, but other grains, as well as beans, lentils and peas, benefit from being combined so that their deficient amino acids will supplement one another (p. 55). Or, serve a deficient protein with a complete one such as eggs, milk or cheese. Legumes themselves will meet your protein needs only if you eat them in vast quantities, and you don't want to do *that*.

111

Bulgur

Bulgur wheat is far and away my favorite grain. I could live on it. Occasionally I meet another bulgur freak, and we talk on and on about its unappreciated virtues. It is a form of precooked cracked wheat that reconstitutes quickly. I prepare it by browning an onion and several cloves of garlic (chopped and mashed, respectively) in 2 tablespoons oil over medium heat. Then I add a cup of bulgur and brown it for several minutes. When it is lightly toasted, I pour in a cup of boiling water, stock or broth, cover the skillet, and lower the heat. Over the next twenty minutes, I gradually add another cup of hot liquid. The bulgur is done when all the liquid is absorbed. Season with tamari.

Fried bulgur makes a wonderful breakfast or lunch the next day. Chop another onion and a green pepper if you have it, mash several more cloves of garlic, and sauté them for several minutes in 2 tablespoons oil over medium heat. Then add the cooked bulgur, and sauté it for several more minutes. Beat up several eggs with a few good dashes of tamari, and pour them into the pan. As soon as the eggs start to thicken, scramble them with a fork, and serve with more tamari on the side. Sliced scallions or a handful of sprouts are good additions along with the eggs.

Wheat Berries and Rice

1 cup wheat berries (whole wheat kernels)	2 cloves garlic, mashed
4 cups water	½ teaspoon thyme
1 cup brown rice	½ teaspoon sage
1 teaspoon salt	½ teaspoon caraway seeds
2 tablespoons butter or oil	¼ teaspoon oregano
1 onion, chopped	1 cup raisins, soaked for an hour and well drained

Place wheat berries and water (including raisin soaking water) in a saucepan, and bring to a boil. Cover, reduce heat, and simmer 15 minutes. Add brown rice. Bring to a second boil, cover, reduce heat, and simmer 45 minutes, or until both are tender. Add salt.

In a skillet, heat butter or oil, and sauté onion and garlic for several minutes over medium-high heat. Add wheat berries, rice and seasonings and stir for two or three more minutes to brown. Add raisins, and sauté all together for 5 more minutes, stirring frequently.

Darrel, High Ridge Farm, Oregon

Note: Darrel orginally made this with soft wheat kernels, but hard wheat berries may be used instead.

Judith's Rice

I asked Judith, the illustrator, whom I met at High Ridge Farm, what I should say about her. She wrote back: "You can tell about my drawing table tucked away in the canning storage room, where I sat and sweated all summer, visiting with people when they came in to put stuff in the freezer or on the shelves. Bags of rice and oats piled around me, I listened to the bubbling gurgle of John's beer brewing and saw through a knothole people working on projects in the shop on the other side of the wall. I had really good talks with people through that wall. It seems that some things can best be said when you can't see the person you're talking to. Engrossed in hand work, people can divulge secrets and be candid with more ease.

"(I also eavesdropped on some really good conversations when people on the other side of the wall didn't know I was there.)"

¼ cup oil
¼ cup tamari
2 onions, chopped
2 cloves garlic, mashed

½ cup soy grits (see note)
2 cups broccoli, chopped
2 cups cooked brown rice

Heat the oil and tamari in a skillet or saucepan. Add onions, garlic and soy grits, and sauté over medium heat for 3 minutes, stirring occasionally. Then add broccoli, and stir-fry for 7 minutes. Add rice and stir to brown. Serves 4.

Note: Soy grits are to soybeans what bulgur wheat is to wheat berries—cracked toasted soybeans. They need only to be reconstituted, being precooked, and may be freely added to various dishes as a supplement.

Several sliced scallions would make a good addition to this dish, added along with the rice. I made it with crude peanut oil, which added a lovely flavor.

Dale's Dhal

Dale was visiting the Clearing—land shared in-
formally by a couple with their friends—when I met
her on Vancouver Island. The couple had gone away
for several days, and I was told I could stay in their
tent. No sooner had I fallen sound asleep than they
arrived home. Like Goldilocks, I leaped out of their bed,
full of alarm and apologies. They recovered from their
equal astonishment and directed me to an A-frame
nearby. There I found Dale. Now wide-awake, I talked
to her, and learned that her home was a beach on the
rugged, sparsely populated west coast of the island.
She lived on top of a cliff behind the roots of a great
fallen tree whose crown lay on the sand far below. The
beauty of the remote place, the awesome view from the
cliff top, compensated for its exposure to the wind and
rain. The year before, she'd lived in a commune. The
group had taken a job planting trees in the northern
part of British Columbia. For a month, Dale cooked
over a campfire. She would often make Chapatis (p.
142) for dinner, fill them with this dhal, and roll them
up.

1 cup lentils	1 teaspoon ginger or finely
Oil	chopped gingerroot
2 onions, halved and sliced	Cayenne
3 cloves garlic, mashed	Salt
4 teaspoons curry powder	

Soak lentils overnight in water. Drain well, saving
water for some other use. In a skillet, heat 1/4 inch oil,
and sauté onions and garlic for 10 minutes over
medium heat with curry, ginger and a good dash of

cayenne. Add the lentils (Dale says, "Throw a dill seed in the oil and when it pops, add the lentils"), lower heat, cover, and sauté 25 minutes, or until lentils are done, stirring occasionally. Salt to taste at the end. Serves 4.

Dhal II

This version was given by the wife of a professor who was in New Mexico doing research on alternative communities. It came, she said, from a mountain community of uptight intellectuals whose location she had promised to keep a secret.

4 cups water
2 cups lentils
2 onions, chopped
1 large carrot, grated
3 cloves garlic, mashed

1½ tablespoons curry powder
1 teaspoon salt
⅛ teaspoon black pepper

Bring water to a boil in a saucepan. Add all ingredients except salt and pepper, stir, bring to a second boil, cover, lower heat, and simmer 40 minutes. Season with salt and pepper. Serves 8.

Note: Lentils need not be soaked, although this shortens cooking time.

Ron's Motherfucker Beans

My friend Robert Houriet met Susan and Ron when he was visiting New Mexico for his book about communes, *Getting Back Together*. They were living at a now-defunct commune started by the Motherfuckers, a radical group from New York. Robert invited them to visit him in Vermont. He invited a lot of people, in fact, but Susan and Ron actually came and stayed for a month. Now homesteading in West Virginia, they're remembered for many things, especially Ron's cooking. He is a burly jack-of-all-trades from Oklahoma who, legend goes, once rode with the Angels. These beans are very extreme.

2 cups dry beans (navy, soldier, pinto, etc.)
4 onions, chopped
A piece of salt pork or bacon (optional)
¼ cup cider vinegar
2 small cans or 1 large can tomato paste

1 cup molasses (see note)
2 tablespoons honey
1 teaspoon Worcestershire sauce
1 teaspoon dry mustard
½ teaspoon cumin
2 cloves garlic, mashed

Soak beans overnight in water to cover. Combine in a heavy pot with two of the onions and the salt pork or bacon and cover with water, including the soaking water. Bring to a boil over medium heat, reduce heat, cover and simmer until tender. Add more water if the beans become too dry.

Place in a baking dish, or combine with the remaining ingredients, including the other onions, in the same pot. Cover and bake two hours in an oven preheated to 325°. Uncover, and bake another half hour. Serves 8. Good reheated.

Note: If you use blackstrap molasses, substitute honey for half of it and omit the additional honey.

Joycie's Millet

1 cup millet
3½ cups boiling water
2 onions, chopped
2 cloves garlic, mashed
1 teaspoon mixed herbs

1 cup raw peanuts or nuts
2 tablespoons oil
Tamari

Add millet to boiling water, cover, reduce heat, and simmer 1-1/2 hours (see p. 73). Meanwhile, sauté onions, garlic, mixed herbs (go lightly on strong-flavored ones such as thyme, tarragon and sage) and peanuts or other nuts in oil over medium heat until browned. Add to cooked millet. Season to taste with tamari.

Joycie, Holy Earth, California

Curried Millet

3 tablespoons butter or oil   ½ cup raisins
2 onions, chopped   1 tablespoon curry powder
1 cup millet   3½ cups water
1 carrot, grated

Heat butter or oil in a saucepan, and sauté onions and millet until browned over medium heat. Add remaining ingredients. Bring to a boil, cover, lower heat, and simmer 1-1/2 hours. Serves 4.

Grady, New Mexico

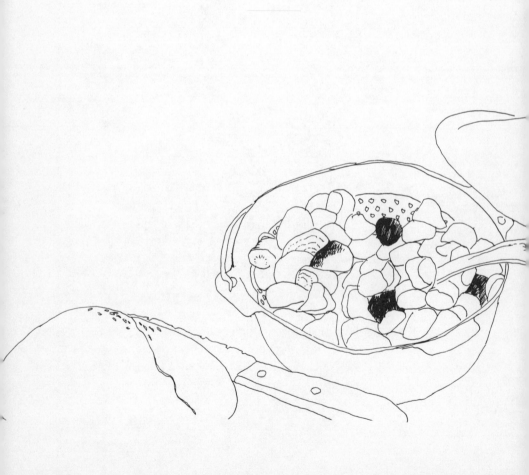

VI. Vegetables

I'd been fond of vegetables, but communes showed me a new dimension of feeling for them. A well-tended vegetable garden yields inconceivable quantities. Commune cooks are vegetable architects who've learned to erect massive meals on a vegetable foundation. Take away food stamps, trust funds, outside jobs—as long as a commune has its vegetables, self-sufficiency remains a plausible goal. Visit a country commune to witness the apotheosis of the vegetable; then enjoy the unusual recipes that follow.

Sweet-and-Sour Beet-Carrot Sauté

The flavors in this recipe are absolutely remarkable. You may use all beets or all carrots instead, but the combination is superb and beautiful to look at as you prepare. If the beets are well scrubbed, they do not have to be peeled.

3 tablespoons oil
2 beets, sliced
2 carrots, sliced
2 onions, halved and sliced
¼ cup raisins

2 tablespoons honey
2 tablespoons vinegar or lemon juice
2 tablespoons tamari
2 cloves garlic, mashed

Heat oil in skillet and stir-fry the beets, carrots, onions and raisins for several minutes over medium-high heat. Add the remaining ingredients, lower heat, toss well to combine, cover, and steam until the vegetables are tender, 15 or 20 minutes. Serves 4.

The Motherlode, Oregon

Cabbage, Cucumbers and Pears

Walter and I fell in together on the way east from Colorado. A serious young man who described himself as "a bicyclist by nature," he was out to see the East Coast for the first time before being drafted (his lottery number being something like 8). Together we survived a ride across Nebraska in a gigantic semi, whose driver picked us up to keep him awake and then met our attempts at conversation with "yup" and "nope." A rainy evening was coming on when two longhairs in a pickup truck stopped for us out of sympathy, although it was a severe inconvenience to have four of us jammed into the narrow cab. The two were headed for the Foundlings, the commune in eastern Iowa where they lived. Once again the Flow had brought me what I wanted when I least expected it. We drove on and on and arrived, dazed, at three in the morning. It was Walter's first commune and my thirty-somethingth.

The next morning I saw that the comfortable old rented farmhouse which held the commune, ringed with trees and lawn, formed an island in the corn running to every horizon. Here and there among it sat other farmhouses, some quite near. A farmer leased the barn in back for a pack of smelly, squealing pigs. Within their green circle, however, oblivious to pigs and curious neighbors, the family lived peacefully. Several of the young men belonged to a jazz-rock band that practiced almost constantly in the living room and got occasional gigs playing at local high school dances. In the kitchen, as in every other country commune, a canning operation was in progress to put up the abundant harvest. I was glad Walter's first commune was so purposeful and harmonious, characteristics I could tell he would value.

In the afternoon I went for a walk in the surrounding corn. It was sturdy as bamboo and depressingly regimented, and I almost got lost in its sameness. Climbing the fence back in, I came on a thickly hung pear tree. Perhaps it was once the pride of a farmer's wife. Cher, the only member from California, was inspired by the pears to invent the following unique recipe.

2 tablespoons oil	2 firm, ripe pears, cubed
2 cucumbers, cut into half-inch cubes	1 tablespoon honey
	¼ teaspoon nutmeg
¼ medium cabbage, sliced into shreds	4 cloves

Heat oil in a skillet, add cucumbers and cabbage, and stir-fry 5 minutes over medium heat. Add pears, honey, nutmeg and cloves ("one for each direction," says Cher), and stir to mix. Lower heat, cover, and simmer 5 more minutes. Serves 4.

Note: Supermarket (nonorganic) cucumbers are waxed and must be peeled. Notice that homegrown cucumbers do not shine.

Sue's Cabbage and Onions

This subtly flavored dish is the creation of the same Sue formerly of the Pride Family whom I met in Vermont.

2 tablespoons oil	2 cloves garlic, mashed
½ medium cabbage, sliced thinly	¼ teaspoon basil
2 onions, halved and sliced	¼ teaspoon tarragon
2 tablespoons sesame seeds	2 tablespoons tamari

Heat oil in a skillet, and stir-fry cabbage, onions and sesame seeds over high heat for three or four minutes. Add garlic and herbs, and lower heat to medium. Stir-fry several more minutes. Add tamari, and stir. Cabbage should still be crispy. Serves 4.

Smokestack's Sweet-and-Sour Carrots

The man who gave me this recipe, sitting in the field in front of the Salwaka General Store in Oregon drinking beer with several friends, didn't want to tell me his name. Instead, he suggested I call it after his horse, Smokestack.

1 cup water	2 oranges
2 unscraped carrots	2 lemons
2 potatoes in their jackets	¼ cup honey

Bring the water to a boil in a saucepan, and add the carrots and potatoes. The carrots must be cut into several pieces to fit. Bring to a boil again, lower heat, cover, and steam 40 minutes, or until the potatoes are tender. Save the water. Cool the potatoes and carrots, and slice thinly without peeling.

Preheat oven to 350°. Line a baking dish with the sliced vegetables. Cover with oranges and lemons, peeled and thinly sliced (the peels add flavor, but they also carry poisonous crud, like most American produce). Combine the vegetable cooking water and the honey, and pour over. Then bake for 30 minutes. Serves 4.

Note: John of High Ridge Farm saw this recipe in my book and improvised his own version. Instead of precooking the vegetables, he cut them up, put them in a baking dish, poured over them a mixture of equal parts of orange juice, vinegar, honey and oil, then baked them until they were tender.

Husk-Steamed Corn

I learned an excellent method of preparation for corn at Sunflower Farm in Ontario (p. 130). Place the unhusked corn in 1 inch water, cover, and bring to a boil over medium heat. When the water boils, the corn is done. Shuck the corn at the table or, if you're afraid the chance of coming upon a defective ear will upset anyone at your table, just before serving. It's hot work, husking steaming corn, but leaving the husks on helps retain nutrients and flavor, and if the corn has to stand a bit before serving, it won't lose flavor.

Posole

Just a few rows of corn can produce a phenomenal yield. Hang your surplus ears around the house, and grind the dried kernels into meal or try cooking them this traditional Indian way, which I learned from Breadloaf's nearest neighbors. They say you can cook dried field corn (the type grown for animal fodder) or feed-store kernels by this method, but the most nutritious variety is said to be multicolored Indian corn, favored by New Mexico communes. Imprinted in my memory is an image of coming down to the pueblo courtyard from the Pit House at Breadloaf one morning and seeing in the shimmering clear light rows of Indian corn freshly hung on a mellow plastered wall: slate, olive, sea green, periwinkle blue, ivory, beneath dusty bundled husks.

To 1 quart dried corn kernels, add 1 cup of sifted wood ashes (preferably hardwood, according to Laura Ingalls Wilder's *Little House in the Big Woods*). Cover with water, and soak 24 hours, or until kernels split.

Cover the corn with fresh water or chicken broth (you can make broth as you cook the corn by adding chicken bones to the water), and bring to a boil. Lower heat, and simmer 2 or 3 hours, or until the corn is tender.

Cucumbers with Mint

Lines (short for Caroline), the girl at Dulusum Farm in Oregon who passed this recipe on to me, learned to cook cucumbers this way in Turkey, where she and her husband had served in the Peace Corps. The commune people she had met since her return reminded her, she said, of Peace Corps volunteers.

3 medium cucumbers
1 cup water
4 tablespoons butter
3 tablespoons whole wheat flour
Salt and pepper
1 egg yolk

¼ cup heavy cream or evaporated milk
2 tablespoons finely chopped fresh mint or 2 teaspoons crumbled dried mint

Peel cucumbers, and cut into inch-thick slices. Place in a saucepan with the water, and bring to a boil. Remove from heat, drain, and reserve stock.

Melt butter in saucepan over medium heat, add flour, cook 1 minute, stir until smooth, and then gradually add the cucumber stock (or liquor, as Lines enticingly calls it). Stirring, bring to a boil. Add cucumbers, salt and pepper to taste, lower heat, and simmer until the cucumbers are tender, about 15 minutes.

Combine yolk and cream or milk. Remove cucumbers, and add the cream mixture and the mint. Blend carefully. Serves 4 to 6.

Note: You may also cook summer squash or zucchini by this method.

Latkes

These must be a real commune special, because I
was given three recipes for them, one by Herman at the
Moon Garden, one at Atlantis in Oregon (a quantity
recipe from their comic book (p. 51) which called for
10 pounds potatoes), and a third by Strell of Elfhome in
New Hampshire. I first heard of Strell at Evenstar in
Oregon (p. 202). The family there, who had migrated
from the hills around Goddard and Franconia colleges,
two outposts of freakdom in Vermont and New
Hampshire, said I shouldn't miss Strell's "egg-leavened
garlic-flavored potato pancakes." Strell, a thoughtful
man who is to some extent the backbone of his faltering
community (it occupies land owned by a girl who
doesn't especially want it there), was surprised when I
showed up and asked for the recipe, particularly since
he doesn't put egg in his latkes. Others do, though, so I
have added an optional egg to Strell's recipe; it adds a
dash of protein and helps hold the mixture together.

2 large or 3 medium potatoes in their jackets, grated	¼ cup whole wheat flour
1 carrot, grated	1 egg, beaten (optional)
1 onion, grated	1 teaspoon salt
2 cloves garlic, mashed	¼ teaspoon black pepper
	Oil

Combine all ingredients except oil, working fast to
avoid deterioration of the vitamin C in the potatoes
caused by exposure to the air. (Adelle Davis suggests
chilling vegetables before cutting or grating them to
slow down harmful enzyme action.) Heat 1/4 inch oil in
a skillet over medium-high heat. When the oil is good
and hot, drop the latkes in by large spoonfuls. Cook
quickly until browned, turning once. Drain quickly on
paper before serving. Traditional accompaniments are
sour cream or applesauce.

T.A.'s Potato Volcano

Two summers ago grasshoppers threatened the potato crop at High Ridge Farm in Oregon, so to save them a number of potatoes were harvested prematurely. To use some up, T.A. boiled them in their jackets, mashed them without peeling, and on a baking sheet fashioned a twin-peaked volcano. He filled the depressions in the centers with sautéed vegetables (lots of onions and garlic would go well in this) and grated sharp cheese in alternate layers. The "slopes" were decorated with more grated cheese and pea boulders. The volcano was placed in a hot oven to melt the cheese; then sprigs of dill were added to forest the slopes below the timberline. As T.A. tells it (John looked in my notebook and remarked, "Bullshit, I don't remember that"), nobody could bear to eat something so beautiful. The father of one of the women was visiting, and he ran and got his camera. Then, after a suitable period of admiration, everyone dug in.

High Ridge Potato Salad

I arrived at Terra Firma in Oregon exhausted. It was hot, and I'd hiked a long way up the empty road. Finding the commune was no trouble—I recognized it immediately by the junked cars and trucks in front and a glimpse of a woman in an ankle-length dress crossing the yard. Sweat dripping into my eyes and steaming my glasses, I staggered toward the farmhouse. From the porch, a figure rose, shouting incredulously, "*Lucy!*" It took me a moment to realize this was Ted, a Berkeley sophomore who'd been spending the summer hitching

around. He'd been staying at High Ridge Farm, far to
the south near the California line, when I left there ten
days before. I caught my breath, drank some water,
and asked for the news from the farm. "Too bad you
left when you did," he commented rather smugly. "You
should have seen what they had for dinner the next
night!" A tested, delicious rendition of how he thinks it
was made follows.

4 medium potatoes in their jackets	¼ teaspoon pepper
1/3 cup oil	Salt
½ teaspoon basil	Mayonnaise
½ teaspoon tarragon	4 scallions, chopped (including some of the green part)
¼ teaspoon rosemary	Herbs (optional)
¼ teaspoon dried dillweed, or	1 clove garlic, mashed
¾ teaspoon snipped fresh dill	(optional)
3 cloves garlic, mashed	

Preheat oven to 425°.

Quarter medium potatoes (or cut large ones into
eighths, small ones into halves) and spread on a baking
sheet with a rim or in a large baking dish. Combine oil,
herbs, garlic and pepper. Pour over the potatoes and
toss them to coat. Bake until the potatoes are tender,
about 40 minutes, basting often. Serve with mayonnaise, preferably homemade, to which have been
added scallions and, if you wish a more pronounced
flavor, a few pinches of herbs and a mashed clove of
garlic. Serves 4.

Pumpkin and Cheese

Sunflower Farm was magnificently situated on a
hilltop in rolling Ontario maple country, now tinged

with autumn. I dreaded arriving with four others
where one could barely expect a welcome, but such
was my fate as a hitchhiker; I was grateful for the ride.
As we pulled in, I noted a rambling farmhouse, a fine
old barn and, beyond, an unfinished geodesic dome. (I
wonder why so many domes are left unfinished? Like
junked cars and big dogs, they were a theme that ran
through my trip.) Jesse and Marjory, standing in the
yard, united in a blank look that confirmed my
paranoia. Later I learned that while the famous farm
(I'd heard of it in Colorado, Oregon, New Mexico) had
once been a haven and crashpad for hundreds of
longhairs, mostly from the Toronto area, the family
was now firmly down to six. When newcomers arrived,
Jesse said, he was so gruff with them that they split in a
hurry. Once he overheard a conversation about
himself in a Toronto restaurant: "Don't go to
Sunflower, man, the vibes there are bad!"—and
realized he'd become a legend.

Nevertheless, when we presented bananas and
cheese and pointed out that we were just passing
through, Jesse softened and welcomed all five of us to
stay overnight. An informed cynic and rationalist (both
he and Marjory held degrees in biology), he immediately began to talk about honey as a fetish. It was
actually no better for you than refined sugar, he said;
their chemical compositions were similar, and both
rotted your teeth and required quantities of B vitamins
for their digestion. Commune people were blind "true
believers" who wanted to think that honey was good
for them, regardless of the scientific evidence. I agreed
he had a good point (p. 185). Then he showed me his
favorite book on nutrition, an obscure, depressing
dental text published in the 1930's which showed
pictures of the teeth of primitive peoples before and

after the arrival of the white man with his white-everything diet.*

Jesse and Marjory also appreciated good food. For dinner, Jesse made the dish below, his own invention, and for dessert, Quick Apple Pie (p. 198). At dinner the couple described the luscious cuisine of Jamaica, where they'd taught for a year. Marjory served a ginger drink she'd learned to make there. She grated a small amount of fresh gingerroot into a teapot and steeped it in boiling water. This peppery tea was served with a touch of honey.

Cut a small pumpkin or part of a large one into 2-inch pieces, and remove pith and seeds. To preserve the vitamins, it would be best to steam the pumpkin in a colander or sieve over boiling water, but Jesse simmered it in 2 inches water, covered, for 40 minutes, or until tender. Then skin the pumpkin, and mash. (If you have very heat-sensitive fingers, you might prefer to peel the pumpkin before cooking with a vegetable peeler rather than touch the hot pumpkin, but I prefer the latter system; the skin comes right off.) Add butter, salt, pepper and as much sharp cheese as you like, cut into small cubes. Stir all together, and serve before the cheese has almost melted. Unusual and marvelous.

Note: Any type of winter squash may be substituted for the pumpkin.

Stir-Fried Radish Tops

The Brush Brook Family in Oregon recommends this

*This book, Nutrition and Physical Degeneration, by Weston A. Price, is reviewed on pp. 152-53 of the Canadian Whole Earth Almanac's Healing issue (Vol. 2, no. 3).

method for preparing radish tops, a green I'd never thought of cooking. It would work well for any greens, dandelion greens, young lamb's-quarters, spinach. These vegetables cook down to a small percentage of their original volume, so use a large pile for even a small group—a couple of quarts for 4 people—which you may chop or tear coarsely. Heat 2 tablespoons oil in a skillet and stir-fry several scallions, chopped (including some of the green part), several mashed cloves of garlic, and your mess of greens for 2 or 3

minutes over medium-high heat. Then cover, and steam
for 2 or 3 minutes. Serve with Tamari Gravy (p. 159), to
which you have added 1/4 teaspoon ginger.

Rutabagas and Apples

The nineteen-year-old girl who gave me this recipe at
a New England commune was very beautiful. Her face
had a medieval quality, with a high, rounded forehead
and dark hair gathered demurely back, while curly
locks fell around her cheeks. Lithe, affectionate, ex-
pressing a self-delighted vitality in every movement,
she was by far the most playful spirit in this collective
of hardworking, policy-oriented idealists. A Brooklyn
childhood had made her a hustler at seventeen. Then
two years ago she came up to the nearby college town
with some men for the weekend. She met one of the
commune's founders and began living with him. He's
gone now, but she is very much part of the family, and
her baby by him has eight enthusiastic parents. So
totally is she acclimated that except for her un-
mistakable Brooklyn accent you'd think she'd always
been a country girl.

2 large rutabagas
2 tablespoons water
1 tart apple, cubed
½ teaspoon salt

⅛ teaspoon black pepper
2 tablespoons butter
  (optional)

Peel the rutabagas, and cut into 1-inch cubes. Steam
them with the water in a covered saucepan over low
heat for 20 minutes. Add apple, and steam another 15
minutes. Mash together with salt, pepper and butter if
desired. Serves 4.

Note: The girl who invented this added a little honey and some cinnamon and nutmeg, but we found it so tasty without these that I've omitted them. You might disagree.

Sprouts

Sprouts—germinated seeds—are rich in vitamins and minerals, and on communes are used both as a salad vegetable and as a supplement added freely to casseroles, stir-fries, egg dishes, soups, even bread. In winter they fill in for fresh vegetables, since they're a good source of vitamin C and B-complex and are grown indoors. Every natural foods cookbook gives directions for sprouting, and so will I. At High Ridge Farm, where they have their basic methods down, the lid is removed from a large jar (a gallon in their case), and a quarter-inch of seeds are added to it. Mung beans produce the bean sprouts of Chinese restaurants, alfalfa seeds are said to be the most nutritious, but any untreated bean or grain—wheat berries, soybeans, lentils, chick-peas—can be sprouted successfully. The top of the jar is then covered with fine netting, an old nylon stocking or a double layer of cheesecloth, secured in place with a rubber band. Water is added to cover the seeds, and they are placed in a warm, dark (light will damage the vitamin C content of the sprouts by precipitating en-zyme action) place overnight. In the morning, the water is poured off through the netting—save it for a soup, as it's full of nutrients, or at the very least feed it to the animals—and the jar returned to its hiding place. The sprouts are rinsed twice a day through the netting, which never needs to be removed, and kept moist by the water which clings to them. After the first night, the seeds should never sit in water. The sprouts will be ready in 3 to 5 days, or when they're an inch or more long. An hour or two before eating, you may set them in the sun to get a spot of green if you wish.*

Terra Firma in Oregon, whose members base their diet on raw vegetables, fruit and seeds, used the same technique and had the most extensive sprouting operation I saw anywhere. Helping hang up a load of laundry, I was puzzled to find a number of nylon stockings. They were full of runs, and besides, the women went barefoot. Later I was shown a cabinet containing nine jars of sprouts, their tops covered with nylon stockings.

Sprouts with Cheese

This dish is rich enough in protein (sprouts contain all the essential amino acids) to serve as a main course. Coat the bottom of a skillet lightly with oil. Add sprouts. Cover them with slices of Cheddar or Jack cheese. Place over a low flame, covered, and heat gently just until the sprouts are heated through and the cheese melts. Sprouts are best served raw so that the unstable vitamins C and E will remain unimpaired, but minimal cooking such as this will cause little damage. Serve with tamari.

Dorothy, Dulusum Farm, Oregon

Winter Squash Ultimate

"I pulled into Conklin, I was feelin' 'bout half past

---

*There's a very thorough discussion of sprouts in *Mother Earth News* No. 12, pp. 46-53.

dead. . . ." Nobody I asked in this small New Hampshire city had heard of Crabapple Corners. It was a
commune of yurts, I explained, small, round wooden
houses that looked like cupcake papers inverted over
short dixie cups. I'd been sure that such an odd place
would be famous locally, but no. At last my ride went
on, and I started off on foot, asking for help as I went. A
boy looked puzzled. "Are they, uh, hippies? Like
outside of society?" he asked. "Yes, yes, hippies," I
eagerly agreed. Well, there were some hippies down at
the Pest House. . . . Farther along, a young woman
thought the hippies at the Pest House might be able to
help me. It was growing late, so in desperation I
headed for the place with the grim name, up a wooded
lane just outside town.

No one was home at the neat frame house. A gigantic
Newfoundland wagged his tail as I opened the door
and peered in anxiously. From a poster, John Lennon
reassured me that I'd found the right place, so I sat on
the lawn and watched the dog frolic with a goat while
the sun set. In the last dim light a bearded freak finally
arrived in a pickup truck loaded with wood. My frantic
questions failed to perturb him. Crabapple Corners, he
said, was eight miles away, but Karen, one of its
members, worked at the same home for delinquent
boys as his wife (who arrived home from work later
looking nothing like a hippie in a stunning red suit and
heels). He called Karen, and she in turn suggested that
Jim, another member, pick me up on his way to a
square dance where he would play bass that night,
then take me home to the commune for the night.

While we waited for Jim to come, I asked about the
house's peculiar name. During a smallpox epidemic at
the turn of the century, my host explained, the town
had quarantined the sick here. I was glad to learn that

the name predated the current occupants. Conklin was, after all, the only place in all my travels where a child had jeered "Hippie!" at me on the street.

When Jim the bass player arrived, I found that the goat had gotten into my pack, which I'd left outside, and eaten up the bag of nuts and raisins I'd bought as a present for the commune. Then as we drove to the dance, Jim questioned me keenly. The main purpose of his maneuver, which took him miles out of his way, had apparently been to screen me. Crabapple Corners was small, he remarked, and cherished its obscurity. Ah well; my day had begun with being asked if I were a police agent (p. 29). I must have passed, since the night eventually ended with a night's sleep under the round and fluted roof of a yurt. For a discussion and pictures of yurts, see The Last Whole Earth Catalog, p. 101. This recipe of Karen's is equally far out.

1 small winter squash (1½ pounds)	1 cup rolled oats or rolled wheat
½ cup raisins or currants	¼ cup sesame seeds
½ cup mixed dried fruit (dates, prunes, apricots, apples, figs, etc.) snipped	¼ cup whole wheat flour
	¼ cup oil
½ cup water	½ teaspoon salt
½ teaspoon cinnamon	2 onions, chopped
¼ teaspoon each cinnamon and cloves	2 tablespoons oil
	½ cup sunflower or pumpkin seeds

Bake squash at 350° until soft—about 40 minutes. Cool, peel and mash. Keep oven going.

Combine raisins, dried fruit, spices and water in a saucepan. Bring to a boil over medium heat and boil several minutes. Remove from heat and allow to stand.

Toss together oats or rolled wheat, nuts, sesame seeds, flour, salt and 1/4 cup oil. Spread on a lightly oiled baking sheet, and bake at 350° for half an hour, or until lightly browned, stirring occasionally. Keep oven going.

Sauté onions in 2 tablespoons oil until lightly browned, and add to squash, along with the dried fruit mixture.

Toast sunflower or pumpkin seeds in a dry skillet over medium heat, stirring frequently, until browned.

Oil a baking dish or pie plate. In the bottom, spread the granola mixture. Top it with the squash mixture. Sprinkle with the seeds. Bake at 350° for 20 minutes. Serves 6, and you won't need dessert.

Note: Karen made this with a larger squash—3 pounds or more—and doubled all the ingredients, making two of each layer.

Zucchini is the king of commune summer vegetables. Root and dark-green leafy vegetables are richer in vitamins and minerals, but zucchini grows to enormous size and thrives so readily that everywhere I went I ate and ate and ate it. One night at Breadloaf, I volunteered to make dinner. As usual, forty people were on hand, most of them transients. I decided to use up some leftover tempura batter with one of the giant zucchini, quartered and sliced. A long-haired Japanese boy who'd been hitching around the country asked what he could do to help. I suggested he dip the zucchini slices in the batter and deep-fry them in hot oil and handed him a pair of tongs. Laying them aside, he located a pair of long-handled chopsticks among the utensils. With these he deftly fried zucchini for an hour, while crowds milled around him in the cramped, dirt-floored, dimly lit kitchen, bumping into one another and barking their shins on the stumps that served as chairs. His grace and dedication illuminated that particular dark corner.

Vara's Zucchini

2 tablespoons oil
2 onions, chopped
1½ pounds (about 5 small or
  2 medium) zucchini, unpeeled
  and cut into chunks
2 to 3 cloves garlic, mashed

½ teaspoon basil
½ teaspoon oregano
¼ teaspoon rosemary
1 small can tomato sauce
Salt and pepper

Heat oil in a skillet, and sauté onions over medium heat for several minutes. Add zucchini (or yellow summer squash), garlic and herbs, and stir-fry several more minutes. Pour in tomato sauce, cover, reduce heat, and simmer 15 minutes, or until tender. Season to taste with salt and pepper. Serves 4 to 6.

Vara, Peter Gray's Valley, N.M.

Susan's Dilled Squash

3 tablespoons oil
2 onions, chopped
1½ pounds zucchini, unpeeled
  and sliced
2 tablespoons sesame seeds
2 teaspoons poppy seeds
  (optional)
½ teaspoon celery seeds

½ teaspoon dill seeds
1 tablespoon snipped fresh
  dillweed or 1 teaspoon
  dried dillweed
¼ pound mushrooms, sliced
2 tablespoons tamari
Salt and pepper

Heat oil in a skillet, and sauté onions several minutes over medium heat. Add zucchini, seeds and herbs, and stir-fry 5 minutes. Add mushrooms, and stir-fry 5 more minutes. Pour in tamari, cover, reduce heat, and simmer 15 minutes. Season with salt and pepper to taste. Serves 4 to 6.

Note: The first time I made this, for my friend Richard, he complimented me elaborately in advance, saying, "Having Lucy cook dinner for you is like overhearing Barbra Streisand singing in the shower." Then the squash turned out pallid and bland. The next night I tried it again, and this time I figured out how to bring out the flavors: The seasonings must be sautéed with the zucchini.

Susan suggests that if you prefer the flavor of mushrooms sautéed in butter, do so separately and add them at the end.

Susan, Santa Cruz

Stuffed Zucchini Leslie

Many communes have an outstanding supercook. Leslie was the one at Plate Rock Ranch in California, and on the day I visited she was scheduled to make dinner. She crushed my hopes, however, by remarking that she too planned to write a cookbook. I hung out most of the afternoon in the kitchen, but she never let any of her secrets slip. Dinner was delicious, especially the stuffed zucchini. I had seen her make it, but there was a crucial soupçon of flavor that I couldn't identify. After dinner one of the men gave me a lift to another commune down the road, which was holding its weekly open sauna for the community and where I hoped to spend the night. "Get any recipes?" he asked. "Not a one," I answered casually. "By the way, what made that zucchini tonight so good?"

"Black mustard seed," he answered.

So here, with apologies to Leslie, is my version. I've never found black mustard seed yet, but the common yellow variety works fine.

4 small or 2 medium (about 1 ¼
   to 1 ½ pounds) zucchini
2 tablespoons oil
2 onions, chopped
½ teaspoon whole
   mustard seed

2 cloves garlic, mashed
⅛ teaspoon black pepper
Salt
1 small can tomato sauce

In or (preferably) above 1/4 inch boiling water, steam zucchini 10 minutes. Cool. Cut in half, and scoop out the insides. Chop the pulp. Preheat oven to 350°.

Heat oil, and sauté the onions several minutes over medium heat, along with the mustard seed. Add garlic and zucchini pulp, and sauté 5 more minutes. Add pepper and salt to taste. Put shells on a baking sheet, and fill with the sautéed mixture. Top with tomato sauce. Bake 15 minutes. Serves 4.

Poia

2 cups whole wheat flour
½ teaspoon salt
¾ cup cold water
3 tablespoons oil
6 cups thinly sliced vegetables
   (see below)

2 to 4 cloves garlic, mashed
½ teaspoon caraway seeds
Salt and pepper
Butter
Oil

First, prepare chapati dough. Chapatis are a form of Indian flat bread resembling tortillas and frequently served as an accompaniment to commune meals. Combine flour, salt and water. Knead several minutes to form a soft dough. Form into eight balls and roll each one into a roughly triangular shape.

Heat 3 tablespoons oil in a skillet over medium heat and stir-fry vegetables with the garlic and caraway seeds. Good vegetables include those listed for Couscous (p. 45). For slower-cooking vegetables such as carrots and cauliflower, you may cover the pan after stir-frying for several minutes, lower the heat and steam until tender. Vegetables must be sliced or chopped so they are in fairly small pieces. Salt and pepper to taste.

Place a good spoonful of vegetables on each chapati triangle, top with a small piece of butter, and fold up, pinching to seal. To seal tightly, moisten the edges with a little water. Heat 1/4 inch of oil in a heavy skillet until quite hot and fry the poia until brown, turning once. Or, bake on a baking sheet until browned in a hot oven. Serves 4 to 8 (depending, of course, on whether you eat one or two).

Dale, Vancouver Island

VII. Salads

In summer, salads are served on country communes every night. They are crisp, straight from the garden, the salads of your dreams, the homesteader's payoff.

Robert Welch's Avocado Salad

I met him hitchhiking in California, this fifteen-year-old with the deliciously ironic name. He lived at Morningstar Ranch with his mother, who must be an interesting woman. Robert was the first of many to tell me about Arnold Ehret's Mucusless-Diet Healing System,* which forbids allegedly mucus-forming meats

*Arnold Ehret, *The Mucusless-Diet Healing System* (Ehret Literature Publications).

145

and starches and stresses raw vegetables, fruits, nuts
and seeds. Its object is to purify the body of disease-
forming mucus. This salad is as luscious as it is
exemplary.

2 or 3 ripe avocados, peeled
    and sliced
1 green pepper, chopped
1 stalk celery, chopped
1 red onion, halved and thinly
    sliced

2 ripe tomatoes, quartered
1 cup sprouts (p. 135)
¼ pound fresh spinach,
    coarsely torn or chopped

Combine vegetables with Dressing:

¼ cup tamari
Juice of 1 ½ lemons
¼ cup oil

2 to 3 cloves garlic, mashed
⅛ teaspoon oregano or basil
⅛ teaspoon tarragon

Serves 4.

Guacamole I

Robert Welch must be a natural culinary genius.
This recipe is as unique and good as the last. He
acquired his taste for avocados in Hawaii, where they
reportedly lie a foot deep on the ground.

2 large ripe avocados, pitted
    and peeled
1 green or sweet red pepper,
    minced

1 stalk celery, minced
1 small red onion, minced
⅛ pound mushrooms,
    chopped

Mash avocados, and add the other vegetables. (You
may also add sprouts, or sunflower, sesame or chia
seeds.) Serve with Salsa Fria:

1 small yellow onion, minced
1 green chili pepper, minced
    (p. 23)
2 ripe tomatoes, chopped

¼ teaspoon oregano
¼ teaspoon basil
¼ cup tamari
3 cloves garlic, mashed

Combine in a jar, and shake well. Pour over guacamole. Serves 4.

Robert also described a salad of grapefruit and avocado dressed with honey, currants and cinnamon. You might experiment with that one.

Guacamole II

2 ripe tomatoes
2 large ripe avocados, pitted
  and peeled

1 small onion, minced
½ cup sour cream or yogurt
Juice of 1 lemon

Heat the tomatoes in a pan over high heat, or hold on a long-handled fork over a flame until the skins blacken and burst. Peel. (Or, in the winter, use canned tomatoes.) Combine in a large bowl with avocados and onion. Squish with a bottle (Chuck suggests a beer bottle). The longer you squish, the more together the mixture gets. Add the sour cream or yogurt and the lemon juice, and cover. Let sit several hours to mellow. Serves 4.

Chuck, Breadloaf, New Mexico

Turkish Cucumber Salad

Versions of this abound. The recipe below comes from Turkey via Lines of Dulusum Farm in Oregon. A man named Wide-Mouth Mason at the Tribe in Colorado suggested a variant called Ja-jeek (also from Turkey); it contained mint instead of garlic. A girl I met hitchhiking near San Francisco described a mixture called (she thought) Suzuki. It was Greek and consisted of a quart of yogurt, a grated cucumber and an entire head of garlic, mashed. She suggested it as an accompaniment to spicy foods—as if it were bland!

2 cups yogurt
2 teaspoons fresh dill, snipped,
   or ¾ teaspoon dried dillweed

2 to 3 cloves garlic, mashed
1 large cucumber

Combine yogurt, dill and garlic, and marinate
overnight, chilled and covered. Thinly slice a
cucumber (peeled if it's not organic), and pour the
dressing over it. Serves 4.

Hungarian Potato Salad

Commune people talk about the necessity of ac-
cumulating basic skills—auto mechanics, carpentry,
herbal healing. The serene lady at Crow Farm who
gave me this recipe is said to be a midwife.

4 medium potatoes, boiled
   in their jackets
4 hard-boiled eggs, sliced
4 slices bacon, fried and
   crumbled
½ cup melted butter

½ to 1 cup sour cream
1 teaspoon salt
½ teaspoon paprika
Lettuce
Oil and vinegar dressing

Preheat oven to 350°.
Oil a baking dish and prepare a layer of 2 of the
potatoes, sliced in their jackets, 2 of the eggs, 2 of the
crumbled bacon slices, and half the melted butter and
sour cream, combined. Sprinkle with half the salt and
paprika. Then make another layer. Bake, covered, for
20 minutes. Chill and serve on lettuce with a simple oil
and vinegar dressing. Serves 4.

Sprout Salad

My visit to the True Light Beavers in Woodstock,
New York (p. 102), was nearly a disaster. As a trial run

for my trip, I went out to Woodstock on the bus,
depressingly enough, one Sunday in March and asked
around for a commune, marveling all the while at my
boldness. I was directed to the Beavers, an extended
family living in a former inn. They were very helpful.
This recipe, a gift from friends, was posted on their
refrigerator. Then I saw a new bicycle and asked if I
could take it for a ride. The owner gave me permission
with some reluctance. I glided downhill for several
miles, but when I started back up, the gears stripped,
then the chain fell off, and finally the rear wheel
followed it. I had to carry the bicycle the last mile back.
The unmechanical family was appalled. Luckily a
visitor who had arrived during my ride was able to fix
it, saying that cheap bikes were often sold with in-
sufficiently tightened bolts. I was so relieved, I liked
him and everyone so much, that I talked without
restraint. At last one of the Beavers, a taciturn artist,
remarked, "Do you ever stop talking? You talk more
than any chick I ever met." Of course that stopped me
cold. Months later I read an article in a national
magazine which regretted the rarity of silence in our
world. An interview with the same artist was a feature
of the story. Every Monday, in emulation of Gandhi, I
learned, he remains silent.

3 cups bean (or other)
  sprouts (p. 135)
¼ cup oil
2 tablespoons tamari
2 tablespoons vinegar or
  lemon juice
¼ cup chopped scallions

¼ cup chopped pimiento or
  green pepper
2 tablespoons sesame seeds,
  ground
1 clove garlic, crushed
⅛ teaspoon black pepper

Combine all ingredients. Chill 1 hour before serving.
Serves 4.

Lisa's Super Optional Avocado Dressing

1 tablespoon water
1 ripe avocado (optional)
Juice of ½ lemon
½ cup oil, preferably sesame

1 clove garlic, mashed
Pinch dried or fresh dillweed
1 tablespoon tamari

Mash the avocado and combine it with the other ingredients, or cut it in pieces and whir all the ingredients in a blender. Serve on ripe tomatoes or a green salad. If you omit the avocado and water, you get a lovely light dressing for a tossed salad. Lisa served it in New Mexico (p. 74) in the latter form on a salad of lettuce, alfalfa and lentil sprouts, sliced raw zucchini and turnip, and nuts.

Cream Dressing

Bill, the supercook at Repose in Oregon (the name comes from the I Ching), makes this dressing often because "it's so easy." The difficulty comes in obtaining the cream.

½ cup cream (see note)
¼ cup cider vinegar (see
  note)

1 tablespoon honey
¼ teaspoon paprika
Pinch salt

Combine all ingredients and use as a dressing on a green or cabbage salad.

Note: You may substitute sour cream for the sweet and decrease vinegar to 2 tablespoons.

Debbie's Cheese Dressing

Debbie and her husband, who were homesteading nearby, came to dinner at Prairie Dog Village in California the second night I spent there. Debbie volunteered to make her special salad dressing. "Do you have any blue cheese?" she asked innocently. The answer, unsurprisingly, was no. "Red wine vinegar?" No again. "Olive oil?" No a third time. Reluctantly, she used salad oil, cider vinegar and Cheddar cheese. The result was ravishing.

¾ cup (3 ounces) grated Cheddar cheese
1 cup oil
¾ to 1 cup vinegar (see note)

2 to 4 cloves garlic, mashed
1 teaspoon paprika
½ teaspoon salt
Dash pepper

Combine, and use as a dressing for a green or cabbage salad.

Note: I like tart dressings and could choose the larger amount of vinegar, but I'd recommend starting with the smaller amount and adding vinegar gradually to taste.

Fruit Salad Dressings I, II and III

I. From Marilyn of Vancouver Island: Combine 1 cup yogurt, 2 tablespoons honey and the juice of 1/2 orange. (Use the other half in the salad.)

II. At the Clearing on Vancouver Island, I ate a salad of romaine, grated carrots and chopped apples dressed with a mixture of 1/2 cup mayonnaise, 1 tablespoon lemon juice and 1 tablespoon honey. This dressing with the addition of 1/2 teaspoon curry powder is my favorite for carrot and raisin salad, but we also had it recently with an incredible mixture of cottage cheese, raw cashews, sliced bananas and chopped dates.

III. From the Brush Brook Family in Oregon: "Smash up a banana fine. Add 1 cup yogurt, 2 tablespoons honey, 2 tablespoons raisins, 2 tablespoons sunflower seeds." As well as a dressing for a fruit salad, this is recommended as a baby food (minus the raisins and sunflower seeds) and as a dessert.

The Lord's Salad Dressing

Since I had forgotten to bring my usual gift of cheese to Atlantis in Oregon, I went along on a run down the mountain to the nearest town, fourteen miles away. I sat in the back of the van with three residents of Fat City, a large tent: a hostile young man in an Army jacket, leading a pet gibbon on a leash, a black teenager from Mississippi who had come to Oregon in the Job Corps and dropped out, and a recently divorced photographer in his late twenties who specialized in nude shots. "We're different from Them," the photographer said in a low voice indicating the long-haired driver. "When They're sick, They use herbs. When we're sick, we take four-way cold tablets." The trio were going to town to eat hamburgers in a diner, since the commune's only rule forbade meat on the premises. They also bought popcorn, instant coffee, cocoa and Boone Farm Apple Wine for their tent. On the way back up, the van stopped for Ty, another member. "Don't tell him about the wine," the photographer whispered. He stuffed the groceries in my shoulder bag and added, "Take these to the tent when we get back."

Ty was religious, gentle and a follower of the mucusless diet (p. 145). Remembering Robert Welch, I asked him if he had a favorite salad dressing. He did. "Shall I name it after you?" I asked him as I wrote it down. "You should name it after the Lord," Ty replied.

The morning I left Evenstar, farther south in Oregon, I heard that Ty had arrived during the night. He and a companion had got stranded while hitchhiking in on the back road in and decided to camp overnight. For some unimaginable reason, Ty lay down in the road—by the side, I suppose—where a truck from the commune struck him. Luckily, it was going so slow that his injuries were slight. I left without seeing him. Two months later, in New Mexico, I heard of Ty again. Apparently he was something of a nomad. "He got run over by a truck," I was told, "but he's getting better now."

1 cup oil
1 cup cider vinegar
3 tablespoons honey
3 cloves garlic, cut in half
½ cup tomato sauce
½ teaspoon salt

¼ teaspoon each caraway seeds, oregano, snipped dill (or a pinch of dried dillweed), sage and rosemary

Combine all ingredients in a jar with a lid, and shake well. Allow to steep several hours. Serve on green or cabbage salads.

Sesame Dressing

Joycie, a lovely, smiling sixteen-year-old at Holy Earth in California, suggested this protein-rich dressing. She had recently returned from Hawaii. Now the West Coast felt damp and cold to her, and she dreamed of finding another tropical island where she could live simply, drenched in sunlight. Try this, appropriately, on an avocado salad.

¼ cup sesame seeds
2/3 cup oil
2 tablespoons tamari

2 tablespoons lemon juice
2 cloves garlic, mashed

Use the sesame seeds raw, or toast them lightly in a hot oven or on top of the stove until they start to pop. Grind them, and combine with the remaining ingredients. Or run all together in a blender.

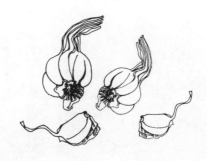

VIII. Sauces

Chili Sauce Piquante

2 tablespoons oil
1 onion, chopped
1 green pepper, chopped
1 stalk celery, chopped
2 green chili peppers,
 chopped (p. 23)
1 tablespoon vinegar
1 tablespoon honey

¼ teaspoon salt
2 cloves garlic, mashed
½ teaspoon basil
¼ teaspoon thyme
¼ teaspoon rosemary
¼ teaspoon sage
2 cups canned or stewed
 tomatoes

Heat oil, and sauté onion, green pepper and celery in a saucepan over medium heat until tender. Add the remaining ingredients, cover, lower heat, and simmer 1 to several hours, adding water if sauce becomes too dry. Serve with eggs, enchiladas, beans or wherever a hot sauce is desired. You may add pieces of leftover meat and serve with rice or beans. Include the chili seeds for a really hot sauce.

Debbie, The Furry Freak Brothers, New Mexico

French Sauce

2 tablespoons butter or oil	½ cup apple juice or cider
2 tablespoons whole wheat flour	Pinch nutmeg
½ cup milk	Salt and pepper

Melt butter or heat oil over medium heat in a saucepan. Stir in flour, and combine. Then add liquids, stirring constantly. Remove from heat, and add nutmeg and salt and pepper to taste. Serve with vegetables such as broccoli or cauliflower.

Micheline, Wheeler's Ranch

Miso Almond Sauce

Finding Crabapple Corners was hard enough (p. 137). Then, when I finally arrived, late at night, I learned that the family's renowned supercook, Karen, had just started on the breakfast shift in the kitchen of a correctional school for boys. To gather her recipes, I had to ride to work with her in the chilly dark of early morning, regretting sleepily that I was never to see the wonderful yurts in the daylight. Instead, while the rising sun gleamed red and small through the window of the chrome-and-Formica kitchen, I watched Karen stir a huge pot of Quaker oats. The idealistic young people hired to staff the kitchen had to use up the mixes and processed products left behind by the last cook before they could change the school's diet over to natural foods. Worse would be contending with the tastes of boys who, like many Americans, were sugar junkies. I recalled the summer I had worked as a cook for an American Friends Service Committee work camp. One night when we ran out of bread, two of the kids rummaged desperately through the kitchen until they found some stale hamburger rolls. Without white bread on the side, they could barely have choked down their dinner.

Miso is a fermented soybean puree, available at natural foods stores, that tastes much like tamari. People who live in yurts are fond of it.

2 tablespoons oil
2 onions, chopped
½ cup chopped almonds
2 tablespoons arrowroot starch
¼ cup miso

2 cups water
2 cloves garlic, mashed
2 tablespoons snipped
   parsley

Heat oil in a saucepan, and sauté onions and almonds over medium heat until browned. Dissolve arrowroot starch in a little of the water, and add along with the remaining ingredients. Heat, stirring, until the miso is dissolved and the sauce thickens. Serve on rice as a main dish or over steamed strong-flavored vegetables.

Tamari Gravy

2 tablespoons oil
2 onions, chopped
¼ cup tamari
1½ cups water

1 tablespoon arrowroot
   starch
⅛ teaspoon black pepper

Heat oil over medium heat in a saucepan, and sauté onions until tender. Add tamari and 1 cup of the water. Dissolve starch in remaining water. When tamari mixture has come to a boil, stir in the dissolved starch and cook until thick, stirring constantly. Season with pepper. Serve over mashed or baked potatoes, sautéed sprouts, peas, rice etc.

Note: You may omit onions, or sauté several sliced mushrooms along with them.

Terra Firma, Oregon

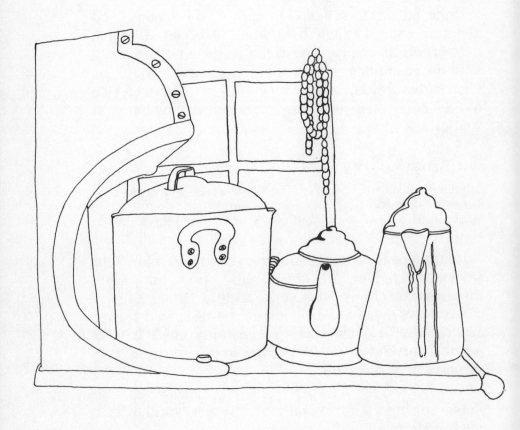

IX. Cereals and Pancakes

I've selected three out of eight recipes for granola — a delicious, easy and popular oat-based cereal. The first is closest to commercial granola, although much better; the second resembles crumbled cookies; the third has its own nutty character. All granolas can benefit from the addition (at the end) of raisins, currants, chopped dates or any other dried fruit.

The simplest granola of all was suggested by a lady who gave me a ride in California. She had eaten it at an ashram in Arizona. Roast rolled oats in a hot oven or on top of the stove in a dry skillet until brown (watching carefully for burning). Mix with sunflower seeds, raisins or currants, a sprinkling of cinnamon and salt. Serve with milk and honey.

Coconut Granola

10 cups rolled oats (see note)   1 cup honey
2 cups wheat germ   2/3 cup hot water
2 cups unsweetened coconut   1½ cups oil
1 tablespoon salt   1 tablespoon vanilla

Mix together dry ingredients. Combine liquid ingredients in a jar or, if the honey is hard, in a saucepan over low heat, and blend. Pour over the dry ingredients; toss well. Spread on oiled baking sheets with a rim and bake at 325° for 45 minutes, or until lightly browned, stirring often. Cool, and store airtight.

Note: You may also add a cup of sesame seeds and/or a cup of sunflower seeds. Rolled wheat or wheat or rye flakes may be substituted in any proportion for the rolled oats in this and the following recipes.

High Ridge Farm, Oregon

Brush Brook Crunchy Granola

3½ cups rolled oats   1 cup wheat germ
2 cups whole wheat flour   ¾ cup warm water
½ cup soy flour   ¾ cup honey
½ cup unsweetened coconut   ¾ cup oil
2 teaspoons salt

Mix dry ingredients and combine liquid ingredients as above. Spread on oiled baking sheets, and bake as above, stirring occasionally. Cool, and break up with fingers. (Walnuts, sesame seeds and sunflower seeds may be added along with the dry ingredients; raisins and other dried fruit may be added afterward.)

Brush Brook Family, Oregon

Peanut Granola

10 cups rolled oats	1 teaspoon cinnamon
1 cup raw peanuts, coarsely chopped	½ cup honey
1 cup sesame seeds	½ cup molasses
1 cup unsweetened coconut	½ cup oil
1 cup fine cornmeal or whole wheat flour	½ cup peanut butter
1 tablespoon salt	½ cup water
	1 teaspoon vanilla
	1 cup raisins or currants

Preheat oven to 325°.

Combine dry ingredients, except raisins or currants. Heat liquid ingredients in a saucepan over low heat, stirring, until the peanut butter melts and all are blended. Pour over the dry ingredients, and toss well. Bake on oiled baking sheets until lightly browned, stirring once after 20 minutes. Add raisins or currants.

Doug, Hill House Foundation
for Centering, Massachusetts

A good breakfast cereal which I saw eaten at the Foundlings in Iowa was roasted salted soybeans (p. 229), served with milk and, for a sweet-and-salty effect, honey.

Whole-Grain Breakfast Cereal

At Earth, Air, Fire and Water in Vermont, I was told to toast whole wheat berries in a skillet over medium heat "until they smell nice" and begin to pop, then crack them in a meat grinder (the finest blade) or a grain mill (set for coarse grind). Cover them with double their amount of water, bring to a boil, cover, lower heat, and simmer until tender and all water is absorbed—about half an hour. This can be served as a breakfast cereal or a grain at dinner. They also suggested combining wheat berries and rice, toasting and cracking them as above, and cooking them together.

Several days later I attended a houseraising at the Black Flag in New Hampshire. The night before, the parents of one member arrived from Queens with 200 kosher hot dogs, a pound of horseradish mustard and a large noodle pudding. Close behind came the entire Milkweed Hill Family from Vermont, who bedded down in the barn for the night. The next day brought a hundred more friends and neighbors, including several local farmers and a nimble elderly carpenter. On the ground lay the framework of an addition to the communal house, meticulously measured and cut beforehand. Traditional barn-beam construction, using mortises, tenons and pegs instead of nails, had been followed. When the beams were up, they fitted together exactly. The frame was raised into place by one team pulling on ropes from the farmhouse roof, another pushing with poles from below. While the house was going up, I helped press cider. Many New England communes keep an old-fashioned cider press into which are fed wormy, bruised windfalls, and if you ask about the worms, you're always told they add protein.

Midday, a buffet of traditional harvest dishes brought by guests was laid out: roasts, hams, coleslaws, pies. Breakfast had also been memorable. Odessa and Jake cracked brown rice in the grain mill and cooked it like whole rice—1 cup rice to 2-1/2 cups water. They set it out with butter, a pitcher of cream from their cow, and a pot of chopped apples tossed with honey, nutmeg, cinnamon, sesame seeds and currants. My friend Robert, who dislikes cooked cereals, declared it the best oatmeal he'd ever tasted.

At High Ridge Farm, yogurt is a popular breakfast. Made fresh every day, incubated in a styrofoam chest filled with 120° water for three hours, then refrigerated overnight, it's eaten with honey, raisins, fruit, sesame and sunflower seeds, unsweetened coconut. Other communes stick with oatmeal (pardon the pun) or pancakes served with honey. I myself prefer thin, eggy pancakes to the kind weighted down by flours like soy, corn and buckwheat. When they're made thin, whole wheat flour pancakes are as light as white flour ones.

Kremsils

This, from Mona of the Motherlode in Oregon, is an old family recipe. Matzo meal might sound like an exotic ingredient, but mothers sometimes send it to their children at the commune for the Passover season, when Jews are supposed to refrain from other types of flour. These are just wonderful.

6 to 8 eggs
2 cups unsalted matzo meal
2 cups milk
½ cup cottage cheese
1½ teaspoons vanilla

½ cup oil
1 teaspoon salt
¼ cup raisins, currants or
    chopped nuts (optional)

Beat the eggs until light. Add the other ingredients, and beat until smooth. Drop by spoonfuls onto a well-oiled griddle, and bake quickly. Watch carefully for burning. Serve with jam, honey or syrup to 4 to 6.

Yeast-Rising Pancakes

1 package yeast
¼ cup warm water
1 teaspoon honey
¼ cup dry milk (preferably
  noninstant)
2 cups warm water or milk

¼ cup honey
¼ cup oil
2 eggs
½ teaspoon salt
2 cups whole wheat flour
2 apples, grated (optional)

Dissolve yeast with 1/4 cup warm water and honey (see p. 25). Add dry milk, 2 cups warm water or milk, honey and oil. Beat in the eggs, gradually add the salt and flour, beating well, and apples if you wish (for a pleasant tang and moisture). Or add any other kind of fruit—blueberries, sliced bananas (my favorite), diced peaches, sliced strawberries, etc. Allow the mixture to rise, covered, in a warm place for 20 to 30 minutes. Drop by spoonfuls on a hot, well-oiled griddle over medium heat. Pancakes are ready to turn when bubbles appear on their surface. Serves 4.

Barbara, The Farm, Wawa, Minnesota

Swedish Pancakes

These, from Nancy of the Moon Garden in Oregon, mother of five blond children, have a delicate custardlike flavor. Be sure to cook them without burning.

3 eggs
2 cups milk
¾ cup whole wheat flour

2 tablespoons oil
1 teaspoon vanilla
1 teaspoon salt

Beat all ingredients together well. Cover the bottom of a small frying pan with oil, and heat over a medium flame. Pour in a little batter, and tip to spread it over the bottom of the pan. Fry quickly on both sides. These are traditionally served in layers with berries and whipped cream, Nancy says, but the usual accompaniments are also good. Also see Spinach Blintzes (p. 52) and Torgerson's Mexican-Italian Blintzes (p. 88).

Scotch Oat Cakes

Marilyn of Vancouver Island (p. 106) befriended the elderly lady next door. Before she died, the lady gave Marilyn an ancient notebook of recipes, written out in an old-fashioned hand on yellowed paper, collected from who knows what sources. This one gives a new use for an old staple.

3 cups uncooked oatmeal   ½ teaspoon salt
1½ cups water   2 tablespoons oil

Combine all ingredients. Drop by large spoonfuls on a hot, well-oiled griddle and fry until browned on both sides. Eat immediately or put in the oven to get crisp. "Good ate with butter and cheese," the old lady notes, or with honey. Makes about 16.

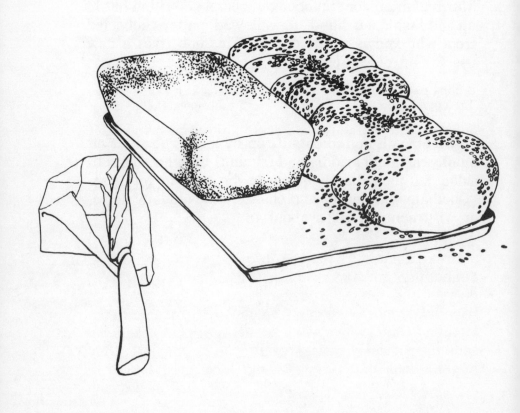

X. Breads, Kneaded and Quick

Communes usually grind their own flour in a table-model mill. At High Ridge Farm they've improved their system by attaching their grain mill to a stationary bicycle. They buy wheat berries, rye berries, soybeans and kernel corn in 100-pound bags at a feed store for very low prices (although these grains are not organic). Hard wheat is ground into bread flour, soft wheat into pastry flour.

Bread need not be baked in pans. At the Hill House Foundation for Centering in Massachusetts, which, despite the imposing name, is a modest group of friendly people living in a farmhouse, I walked into the kitchen to find Doug making twenty loaves of bread. He sells them weekly to a natural foods restaurant. "Say in your book that people should form their loaves in fancy shapes," he suggested. "I made one that looked like a fetus one time." For sandwiches, however, bread kept in shape by a pan is best.

Whether or not to use baking powder is a controversy among commune cooks. The powder contains baking soda, which destroys B vitamins, and "the way we've been brought up makes us nervous wrecks to begin with, without doing anything to make it worse," as Lorraine of Milkweed Hill remarked. The most common brands also contain aluminum compounds. For this reason, some cooks who aren't very far along in the process of switching to all-natural foods use a tartrate type of baking powder (e.g., Royal), aluminum-free. However, once I got into it, I found that yeast can easily be substituted for baking powder in quick bread and cake recipes, so I have eliminated the latter leavening altogether.

Minnesota Bread

A girl I met in New Mexico urged me to visit the commune in Wawa, Minnesota. She came from the state and thought its northern part extremely beautiful. When Walter joined me coming back East, I decided to return to Vermont by way of Minnesota and Canada. We followed the upper Mississippi through Wisconsin, got a ride with Cosmic Bob to the Twin Cities and spent the night there, then after a difficult day reached Wawa. Rides were hard to find. Our best one was with a pretty blond lady from Hibbing who had gone to high school with Bob Dylan. "We thought there was something wrong with him," she said.

As signs of human life appeared more and more

infrequently along the highway, I began to feel haunted. The endless flat, swampy, spindly woodlands seemed terribly desolate to me; in late September the trees were already turning, and almost everyone we spoke to referred half proudly, half with dread to the winters, the hardest, they said, in the continental United States.

The town nearest the commune contained nothing visible but a bar-store combination and a peat moss factory in a large Quonset hut. A quarter mile in from the highway on a dirt road, the rusted hulk of a VW van marked the entrance to the farm. An old white house stared at us hollowly. We went around and opened the kitchen door. A couple seated by the cookstove looked up at us in surprise. "Is this the commune?" I asked.

"It was, but only the three of us live here now," the woman answered, indicating her husband and their little girl. "And we're leaving next week."

The girl who sent me, it turned out, hadn't communicated with the farm in two years. A hard frost struck every month—"I lost my tomatoes in July," Barbara commented wryly—and these last hardy holdouts had finally decided to head for Mexico. Walter and I scavenged for sweaters and jackets in a huge pile of clothes left from commune days. Now, as I write this, I see a forlorn vision of the white house standing dilapidated and empty while snow mounts around it.

We'd got there by sheer ignorant luck but were so unlikely to find a lift out that Barbara and David drove us the next day to Duluth, sixty miles away. In the car, Barbara gave me her bread recipe, which makes more sense than any I've collected. Her method of oiling the

kneading board and her hands to prevent overloading
the dough with flour is especially worth noting.

2 packages yeast (see note)	½ cup dry milk (preferably)
½ cup warm water	noninstant)
1 teaspoon honey	½ cup oil
¼ to ½ cup honey	3 to 5 eggs
2 teaspoons salt	6 or more cups whole wheat
2 cups water	flour

Dissolve the yeast in the warm water with the 1
teaspoon honey. In a large bowl, mix the next five
ingredients well; then add eggs, beating well, and yeast
mixture. Then stir in 1-1/2 cups of the flour, beating
with a whisk if possible. "Beating well as you add the
flour," Barbara says, "is how you develop the glutens
without working your head off." Keep adding the rest
of the flour and beating until the dough is too thick to
beat. Barbara begins with a whisk, proceeds to a
wooden spoon, and ends up kneading by hand. Dough
should be soft enough to "fall around," but smooth. To
prevent the dough from becoming rubbery from too
much flour, as soon as it becomes stiff, stop sprinkling
flour on the kneading board and rub the board with oil.
Keep it covered with a thin layer of oil, and oil your
hands, too. Use this procedure during subsequent
kneadings of the bread when the dough starts to stick.

Place dough in an oiled bowl, turn to oil top, and let
rise in a warm place until doubled. Punch down, knead
("I throw it around the room a few times," Barbara
says), and let rise again. Shape into two or three
loaves, and put in oiled pans. Let rise in pans. For a
crisp crust, whenever dough gets dry while rising in
the pans (the third and final rising), brush with water
or a mixture of water and egg white. Water makes it
crisp, egg white and water very hard. Repeat this

twice during baking, if you wish. Bake at 350° for 50 minutes to 1 hour. If you have oiled the pans very well—at least a teaspoon of oil per pan—the loaves will fall right out when they are done; otherwise they will stick. Makes 2 big loaves or 3 smaller ones.

Note: Barbara buys her yeast in one-pound cakes from a bakery. It's of excellent quality, she says, and economical, but it may take practice to learn how much to use. For this recipe, you would use a piece as big as two supermarket cake-yeast sections.

Jody's Whole Wheat Bread

At Dulusum Farm in Oregon, they told me that the girl who developed this recipe won first prize at the local county fair with it.

½ cup honey	1 cup hot water
2 packages yeast	Whole wheat flour
¼ cup oil	1 tablespoon salt
1 cup warm water	

In a large bowl, place honey and warm and hot water. Sprinkle in the yeast. I killed the yeast the first time I made this by using water that was too hot; the temperatures of both waters together shouldn't exceed 125 degrees, or hot but quite bearable to the touch. Add oil and 2 cups flour and beat a long time— preferably 1,000 strokes—to develop the glutens. Then gradually add salt and approximately 4 more cups of flour, or enough to make a dough that sticks together but isn't too stiff. You may also add whatever else you like at this point—seeds, sprouts, nuts, raisins. Knead 5 to 10 minutes, allow to rise in a warm place, form into two loaves, place in a well-oiled pan, and allow to rise again. When doubled, bake at 350° for 50 minutes to 1 hour. Makes 2 loaves.

Note: Jody makes this with a mixture of wheat germ, soy flour (say, 1 cup of each) and whole wheat flour. I added 1 tablespoon cinnamon with the flour and 1 cup raisins for a marvelous raisin bread.

The classic tests for doneness in bread are if the sides have shrunk away from the pan and if when you turn it out from the pan and tap the bottom, you hear a hollow sound. Determining doneness by sound, however, is a tricky business best learned by experience.

Corn Oat Banana Rye Bread

2 cups cornmeal
2 cups rolled oats
2 cups dark rye flour
1 cup sesame seeds
1 cup wheat germ
2 tablespoons caraway seeds
1 tablespoon salt
2 tablespoons aniseed
5 tablespoons oil
¼ cup molasses

4 cups boiling water
2 packages yeast
½ cup warm water
1 teaspoon honey
3 to 5 very ripe bananas, mashed
1 cup gluten flour (see note)
About 6½ cups whole wheat flour

Combine the first ten ingredients with the boiling water. Let cool. Meanwhile, dissolve the yeast in warm water with the honey (see p. 25). When the first mixture has cooled down, add the dissolved yeast to it along with "3 to 5 very raunchy, black, gooey, yucky bananas—the raunchier the better." (You can hustle overripe bananas in back of the supermarket, or if you're desperate, make your own raunchy bananas by slicing and mashing them and leaving them in the refrigerator for a day or two.) Then add the gluten flour and enough whole wheat flour to make a resilient but somewhat sticky dough. (Kathy uses unbleached white flour for part of this, but I had excellent results with all whole wheat.)

Set to rise in an oiled bowl. Turn to oil top of dough. Cover with a towel, and put in a warm place. When doubled, punch down, knead for several minutes, and shape into 3 loaves. Place in oiled breadpans dusted with cornmeal. Let rise in a warm place until almost doubled. Preheat oven to 400°.

Bake at 400° for 15 minutes, then turn heat down to 375° and bake 30 more minutes. Turn bread out of pans, put back in the oven on racks and turn off heat. Let bread cool down with the oven. (I was of course unable to alter the heat in my wood stove oven, so I baked the bread for 1 hour at a temperature somewhere between 350° and 400° and followed the standard tests for doneness [p. 174] to determine when they were ready to come out.)

Note: "Super extra special bread for after making angel food cake from scratch and having 15 egg yolks left over—beat egg yolks with honey for a long time, till smooth and silky. Use instead of oil. Add after yeast. *Good* yellow rich bread."

Kathy Dutton of Happy Hollow, California, the amazing lady who gave me this recipe and several others, used 4 tablespoons caraway seeds and 4 rounded teaspoons salt. I cut them down, but you might prefer her more pronounced seasonings.

Out on the West Coast, I read a flyer from an association of organic merchants, who pledged not to sell any refined products such as "raw" sugar and white flour. Included on their blacklist was gluten flour, which is wheat flour minus several layers. I leave whether to use it or not in this recipe to your discretion. The purpose of adding gluten flour is to make the bread rise more, since glutens form the structure on which it rises.

Molasses Oatmeal Bread

Communes often have wonderful names. This recipe comes from Sahagiya, a community in Ontario whose name, from an Indian language of the region, means "born together."

1 package yeast
¼ cup warm water
1 teaspoon honey
1/3 cup molasses
2/3 cup water
1 teaspoon cinnamon

1½ cups leftover cooked oatmeal
1 teaspoon salt
About 3½ cups whole wheat flour

Dissolve yeast in the warm water with the honey (see p. 25). Combine all the other ingredients except the flour, and stir into the yeast mixture. Add 2 cups of the flour, and beat very hard for several minutes, to develop the glutens. Then add more flour. Dough should be too stiff to beat, but loose enough so that it "falls around." It will still be sticky. The secret of success with this recipe is not adding too much flour; oatmeal breads quickly become heavy. Knead for several minutes, flouring the board at first, then oiling it. Oil that is worked into the dough will enhance the bread, so be generous.

Place in an oiled bowl; turn to oil the top; then cover with a cloth and allow to rise in a warm place until doubled. Knead again for several minutes and shape into a loaf on a well-oiled baking sheet, or put in a well-oiled breadpan. Cover with a cloth and let rise until doubled. Bake in a preheated 400° oven for 35 to 40 minutes.

Salty Danish Rye Bread

This bread, from the Tribe in Colorado, sounds unbelievable. Rye flour by itself isn't supposed to permit rising, since it lacks the glutens of wheat flour that form a structure for the yeast to raise, but it does. The bread is chewy, moist and flavorful. I have reduced the staggering amount of salt called for by half, but it is still rather salty; you can use less if you prefer. This makes one enormous round loaf.

1½ teaspoons rye flour	3½ cups warm water
1½ teaspoons dry yeast	3 tablespoons honey
½ cup water	2 tablespoons salt
1 package yeast	Rye flour

First, one week in advance, make sourdough starter: mix together 1-1/2 teaspoons rye flour, 1-1/2 teaspoons dry yeast and 1/2 cup water. Let sit all week uncovered in a cupboard.

If you forgot to put up the starter, you may substitute 1 package (1 tablespoon) yeast for it. Otherwise, mix together in a large bowl 1 package yeast, the starter, 1 cup warm water, and the honey. Let stand five minutes, then add salt, the rest of the warm water, and all the rye flour the mixture will take: 9 or 10 cups. If you grind your own flour, grind half of it coarsely and half of it finely. Knead for several minutes. The dough will be somewhat sticky and not like wheat dough. Shape into one or two loaves on a well-oiled baking sheet. Turn to oil the top. Cover with a light cloth (so as not to weigh the dough down). Set it in a warm place to rise until doubled, which could take a couple of hours or all day.

Preheat oven to 450°. Prick dough with a fork all over. Bake one hour, tossing a cup of water on the loaf

every 15 minutes—four cups in all. Then lower the heat
to 325° and bake for another hour. Let cool. "It'll be
hard as a rock, but not on the inside," says the man
who wrote this down for me.

Bagels

Yes, really. Very impressive.

2 packages yeast

2 cups warm potato water
(see note)

1 tablespoon honey

¼ cup oil

4 eggs, slightly beaten

1 tablespoon salt

8 cups whole wheat flour

2 quarts water

Sprinkle yeast over the potato water mixed with the
honey, and let sit 5 minutes to dissolve. Add the
remaining ingredients except the water; mix well; then
knead for 10 minutes. Set in an oiled bowl, turn to oil
top, cover with a towel, and let rise until doubled in a
warm place. Punch down and knead again until smooth
and elastic.

Meanwhile, bring the water to a boil in a large
saucepan or pot.

To form the bagels, divide the dough after its second
kneading into four parts. Roll each part out long in your
hands, and divide it into six portions. Roll each part
between your hands until it's about 6 inches long. Then
wet the ends, and pinch together to form a doughnut.
When the bagels are prepared, drop them into the
boiling water one or two at a time. They will sink to the
bottom, then slowly rise to the surface. As each one

surfaces, turn it and boil one more minute on the second side. Then place on an oiled baking sheet. Bake the bagels at 450° for 10 to 15 minutes, or until golden brown. Makes 24.

Note: Potato water is simply the water in which you've boiled potatoes.

Prairie Dog Village, California

Corn Bread

This recipe, collected at a communal house in Vancouver, is beyond a doubt the best corn bread I've ever eaten. The large amount of oil produces an unforgettable crust.

1 package yeast
¼ cup warm water
1 tablespoon honey
1½ cups cornmeal
½ cup whole wheat flour
½ cup wheat germ

1 teaspoon salt
¾ cup oil
2 eggs
1½ cups milk
2 tablespoons butter or oil

Dissolve yeast in warm water with the honey (see p. 25). Mix together dry ingredients. Stir in the yeast mixture, 3/4 cup oil, eggs and milk. Stir well. Cover and let rise in a warm place for 30 to 45 minutes (depending on how warm the place is and how much time you have).

In a cast-iron skillet, place 2 tablespoons butter or oil. Heat oven to 425°. Put the skillet in the oven until it sizzles or until the butter is melted. Remove, pour in the batter, and replace. Bake until a knife comes out clean—about 20 minutes.

Carrot Bread

The Galaxy Light Movers of Vancouver Island had only recently moved onto land owned by Helen and Bryce, who were homesteading on part of it. Although a barn had been turned into a communal kitchen, most effort was being put into erecting shelter, and everyone took turns going out on a roofing job to support the group. Little time was spent cooking. A Danish girl living in a tepee with her small daughter, a sometime follower of the macrobiotic diet, remarked that she didn't consider food especially important, to a commune or anyone else. I saw an American (the majority of the twelve members came from the United States) making bread without leavening, not because she enjoyed its granite consistency but because it was less trouble that way. The group had a buoyant spirit, however, and their work project is bound to give them the solid financial basis many communes lack. This lovely recipe was brought from California by a member. I balanced things by baking a loaf of it when I returned to California and taking it to the Sunday feast at Wheeler's Ranch.

1 package yeast	½ cup wheat germ
¼ cup warm water	½ teaspoon salt
1 teaspoon honey	2 teaspoons cinnamon
½ cup oil	1 cup grated, unscraped
½ cup honey	carrots
½ cup molasses	½ cup raisins or currants
2 eggs	½ cup chopped nuts
1¼ cups whole wheat flour	

Dissolve the yeast in the warm water mixed with 1 teaspoon honey (see p. 25). Beat together the oil, 1/2 cup honey, molasses and eggs. (Measure the oil first, then the honey and last the molasses. This will prevent the latter two from sticking to the cup.) Combine the dry ingredients, and beat in. Add the carrots, raisins or currants and nuts. Pour into an oiled and floured loaf pan (sprinkle whole wheat flour into a well-oiled pan; shake until it coats the pan; then pour out the excess), and set in a warm place to rise for half an hour, covered with a cloth. Meanwhile, preheat oven to 350°. Bake for 55 minutes, or until a knife comes out clean.

Hush Puppies

Helen, who with her husband opened their land to the Galaxy Light Movers, is a Gemini lady from Alabama. She is dedicated to the preservation of life and forgoes not only meat but eggs, since they are a form of animal life. Her version of this classic Southern recipe has been altered accordingly, without detriment. These crusty deep-fried biscuits are traditionally served with steamed greens or black-eyed peas.

2/3 cup cornmeal   1 small onion, finely chopped
1/3 cup whole wheat flour   ¾ cup milk or water
½ teaspoon salt

Combine all ingredients and drop by spoonfuls into 1 inch of hot oil in a cast-iron skillet. (See p. 24 for advice about deep frying.) Cook until crusty and brown, turning once. Makes about 16.

Yorkshire Pudding

This pudding, based on the same principle as popovers, will astonish you. Though you hardly beat it, it heaves itself up into mountains and valleys and becomes light, airy and crisp. It may accompany dinner as a bread or grain substitute, but Santa Cruz Susan, who gave me the recipe, served it for our breakfast with fresh lemon juice and honey.

6 tablespoons (¾ stick) butter   preferably pastry flour
1 cup milk   4 to 5 eggs
1 cup whole wheat flour,   ½ teaspoon salt

Preheat oven to 400°. Place butter in a small casserole dish, a medium skillet or an 8-by-8-inch baking dish. Set in the oven until it melts.

Meanwhile, combine remaining ingredients in a bowl, and heat until well mixed (no need to overdo it). Add 2 tablespoons of the melted butter; then pour the batter into the rest of the butter. Bake at 400° for 10 minutes; then lower heat to 350° for 30 minutes more, until brown and puffy. In a wood stove, try to keep the temperature between 350° and 400° the whole time.

XI. Cakes, Cookies
and Pies

What to sweeten with or whether to sweeten at all is a universal commune controversy. Although honey is not the perfect substitute for refined sugar we all wish it were,* many communes use it instead, along with molasses and occasionally maple syrup in New England. (Not all: the Evenstar Family in Oregon follows a sound pure-foods diet, but whenever one of them goes into town, he brings back chocolate candy

---

*Honey, it's been remarked, is by nature a processed food. A large dose of any sugar or starch, including honey, raises the blood sugar level drastically, so that an oversupply of insulin is produced to cope with it. In an hour or so, blood sugar plummets to a lower level than before, produing fatigue, irritability, depression. (For a fuller discussion of this syndrome, see Adelle Davis, *Let's Eat Right to Keep Fit*, Harcourt Brace Jovanovich, 1970, pp. 23-24.) Other drawbacks are noted on p. 69. Honey is said to contain valuable minerals and enzymes; but the amounts of the former are generally considered negligible, and the body produces all the enzymes it needs.

bars for everyone.) Others satisfy their craving with fruit—bananas being a great favorite. Desserts are more a luxury than a staple on even the most sweet-loving commune, so when somebody takes the trouble to prepare one, it makes a meal especially festive. Recipes for sweets with redeeming features follow. I hold with substituting honey for sugar, hardly a sacrifice when you consider that honey is the more concentrated sweetener. Whatever its drawbacks, raw honey has the beauty of being a natural food.

Cakes are usually reserved for birthdays, which communes lovingly observe. On mine, June 19, I was at High Ridge Farm, that exquisite place, and when I mentioned it at breakfast, one of the women made a whole wheat cake for me, which she topped with honey and fresh strawberries. I pretended I didn't know it was for me—I'd only been there four days—but I was terribly pleased. That night after dinner an interminable meeting was held, at which it was suggested that the whole group fast for several days, to save money and purify their minds and bodies. I was in suspense, since a fast would have ruined my recipe-collecting. Luckily the proposal was opposed by several members. Afterward, someone finally remembered the cake, and those who were still around sang "Happy Birthday" to me.

Commune cakes are usually taken from standard cookbooks, with whole wheat flour (preferably pastry) substituted for white and honey for sugar. Since honey is more concentrated than sugar, only about half as much of it should be used. The results are inevitably heavier than good old shit cake, but a hearty wholesomeness is imparted that makes the changes taste as worthwhile as they are.

Carrot Cake

1 package yeast	½ teaspoon salt
¼ cup warm water	2 teaspoons cinnamon
1 teaspoon honey	1 cup unsweetened coconut
3 eggs	1 cup finely grated carrot
1 cup oil	1 cup walnuts, chopped
1½ cups honey	1 cup crushed pineapple,
2½ cups whole wheat pastry	well drained (see note)
flour	

Sprinkle the yeast in the warm water with 1 teaspoon honey (see p. 25). Beat together the eggs, oil and 1-1/2 cups honey. Add the yeast mixture. Combine the flour, salt and cinnamon, and blend in slowly. Add the remaining ingredients.

Oil a 9-by-14-inch baking pan, line it with heavy brown paper (you may cut up a paper bag), and oil this too. Pour in the batter, cover with a towel, and set to rise in a warm place for 1 hour. Bake at 350° for 40 minutes.

Note: Use the type of pineapple that comes packed in its own unsweetened juice. Drink what you drain off.

Mona, The Motherlode, Oregon

Apple Cake

½ cup (1 stick) butter	3 to 5 eggs
2 packages yeast	½ cup honey
½ cup warm water	1 teaspoon vanilla
1 teaspoon honey	3 cups whole wheat flour,
½ cup dry milk, preferably	preferably pastry
noninstant	½ teaspoon salt
1½ cups warm water	4 to 6 tart apples, grated

Melt the butter and cool it. Dissolve yeast in 1/2 cup warm water with 1 teaspoon honey (see p. 25). Then add the milk and 1-1/2 cups water. Beat in eggs one at a time. Add 1/2 cup honey, melted butter, and vanilla and blend in flour mixed with salt, along with apples. Pour into a 9-by-14-inch pan, prepared as above. Let rise 30 minutes in a warm place, covered with a towel, and bake in a preheated 325° oven for 40 minutes. This cake is moist and especially good when fresh.

Barbara, The Farm, Wawa, Minnesota

Carob Cake

They were still talking about this cake, freely adapted from *The Settlement House Cookbook*, when I came to Peter Gray's Valley in New Mexico. It had been made the week before for one of the Virgos. Everyone agreed that the carob frosting they'd used had been too rich, and cream cheese was suggested as an alternative. Or try Peanut Butter Frosting (opposite)—delicious.

¾ cup carob powder
¾ cup honey
1 egg beaten
½ cup milk
½ cup butter
½ cup honey
2 eggs
1 package yeast

1 teaspoon honey
¼ cup warm water
2 cups whole wheat flour,
   preferably pastry
½ teaspoon salt
1 cup sour cream or yogurt
1 teaspoon vanilla

Combine the first four ingredients in a saucepan, and heat very carefully, stirring constantly, until the mixture thickens. Remove from the heat and cool.

Cream together the butter and 1/2 cup honey. Add 2 eggs, and beat well. Dissolve the yeast in the warm water mixed with 1 teaspoon honey (see p. 25), and beat in.

Combine the flour and salt, and stir in alternately with sour cream or yogurt. Add vanilla. Beat well. Pour into two cake pans, prepared as for Carrot Cake (above), or a 9-by-14-inch pan. Set to rise in a warm place, covered with a towel, for 1 hour. Bake at 350° for 30 minutes.

Peanut Butter Frosting

The same Suzy who looked at my collection and justly remarked that I should get rid of all those recipes calling for cans of this-and-that (p. 64) made a large birthday cake for a Virgo at Breadloaf, quadrupling a cookbook recipe for spice cake with the usual substitutions. I went into Taos for the ingredients. "Should I get butter?" I asked her. She glanced around to see if anyone was listening. "No," she replied softly. "Get the cheapest margarine!"

She frosted the cake with a mixture of peanut butter, carob powder and honey. When I made the frosting, I found that since our honey had begun to crystallize, I needed to add milk to make it spreadable (although water would have done). Proportions don't matter; just blend to taste, being sure to sift the lumps out of the carob powder before you add it. The mixture will harden on standing, so make it fairly runny.

Honey Macaroons

4 cups rolled oats (see note)
1 cup wheat germ
1 teaspoon salt
2 teaspoons cinnamon
1 teaspoon nutmeg
1 teaspoon allspice

1 cup oil
1 cup honey
1 teaspoon vanilla
1 teaspoon almond extract
1 cup chopped nuts

Preheat oven to 375°.

Combine dry ingredients. Mix liquid ingredients, and pour over. Add nuts. Drop on a well-oiled baking sheet by spoonfuls, or form into small balls (a sticky business) and press flat with the heel of your hand. Bake until lightly browned—10 to 15 minutes. Be careful not to let them overbrown, as wheat germ will. Makes about 50.

Note: Rolled rye or wheat or rye or wheat flakes may be substituted in any proportion for the rolled oats.

Evenstar, Oregon

Cher's Tea Cakes

As Walter and I were leaving the Foundlings in Iowa, Cher ran out of the house and handed us an Irish blessing for travelers which she had written out. "May the road rise to meet you," it began, and concluded, "And until we meet again, may God hold you in the palm of His hand." Cher makes these exquisite Russian cookies at Christmas and sends boxes of them to friends.

1 cup (2 sticks) butter
2 tablespoons honey
2¼ cups mixed flours (see note)
¼ teaspoon salt
1 teaspoon vanilla

¾ cup finely chopped nuts
Honey, mixed with a little
    water
Unsweetened coconut

Bring butter to room temperature; then cream with 2 tablespoons honey. Add flour, salt and vanilla. Stir in nuts. Chill an hour or more.

Preheat oven to 375°. Roll into balls about 1 inch in diameter. Place on ungreased baking sheets. Bake 10 to

12 minutes, or until lightly browned. Cool. Cookies will be crumbly when they're hot but will harden up as they cool. Dip carefully first in watered-down honey, then in coconut. Makes about 50.

Note: Cher uses a mixture of oatmeal, brown rice and buckwheat flours. I made them with half whole wheat and half brown rice flours. Of course, you could use all whole wheat flour; pastry flour would be best.

Peter Gray's Valley lies hidden in the arid hills not far from Taos. Only vehicles with four-wheel drive can negotiate the road to the top. I hiked in over a horse trail, scrambling up and up and stopping every few minutes to rest, only to descend a path so steep that I couldn't enjoy the relief for thinking of having to come up it again. Then I entered the valley. A glorious chorus burst into song in my head as I walked through the lush grass to drink from a rolicking irrigation stream. Beyond, a musical little river dashed through the valley's two green acres. I could see miniature gabled houses and A-frames tucked here and there; two more, hidden from view, were improbably set above the almost vertical canyon walls.

I entered the sunken, dirt-floored main house. Inside, Peter Gray and several other members (there were thirteen in all, plus one toddler) lingered over a late breakfast. They welcomed me to their diminutive paradise and offered recipes for dog (p. 196) and Peter's "real funky" grape wine, made in two weeks. It tasted bready, he admitted, but it didn't cause fights.

That night they were having their annual wiener roast, with s'mores (a Girl Scout favorite—toasted marshmallows between squares of chocolate and graham crackers) for dessert. ("Of course, we never

do this," they emphasized.) Then on Sunday would be their second annual pie-baking contest. I had planned to go to Colorado that weekend' for an equinox peyote meeting, but I asked one of the girls to throw the I Ching for me. It advised me to take things slow. I stayed.

On Thursday, I started for Taos with several members to buy supplies for the Valley's pies. The car broke down on the way. After wasting the day in a vain attempt to get it fixed, we walked home four miles emptyhanded. The next day we woke to an all-day snowstorm, although it was only mid-September. Choppin, a gentle boy from Texas, and I volunteered to make another desperate run for the supplies, driven by a neighbor from the next valley over. The three-mile dirt road out to the highway from his valley was sheer mud. The men got down in the muck and put on chains, but we still slipped and slid and bogged down several times. Once a passerby pulled us out with his pickup truck; the other times we pushed. On the way back, the car got mired in for good, so we carried the groceries the last mile.

Saturday, the family baked all day. Since the one thing we'd forgotten to buy, it turned out, was pie plates, the Valley bakers made their pies in skillets, cake pans, bread pans. Peter Gray's pie was the most elaborate. He cracked prune pits, extracted and crushed the almond-flavored kernels, and made a liquor by boiling them with poppy seeds and water. This he incorporated into a whipped cream pie from *The Joy of Cooking.* By dinner the smells from the kitchen were so maddening that like children on Christmas Eve who can't wait for tomorrow, the family demanded pie for dinner. Two were offered up, including a pecan pie baked by the eleven-year-old daughter of early-arriving guests.

After a day of snow, then one of rain, Sunday turned out clear and warm. A hundred guests arrived from all over the region, including groups from the Furry Freak Brothers and the Hog Farm. More than forty pies were laid out on an outdoor table. The crowd milled around it. "Their pie consciousness is high," Sunny of the Freak Brothers summed up, but nobody, least of all the Valley family, knew what the procedure for judging and eating the pies was to be. Although we had bought 150 paper plates, no one thought to bring them out. At length, when the suspense grew too great, an orgy of pie-scarfing erupted, with pies being passed from hand to hand while hunks were grabbed out of them. Since nobody got to taste all the pies, the prizes—a pair of silver chopsticks and a cashmere muffler—went unawarded. The neighbor who'd driven us to Taos, a black South African student dropout, awarded himself the muffler on the grounds that his entry, a shepherd's pie, was the only pie with either meat or grass in it.

After all that, I didn't collect any pie recipes at the contest, what with the chaos and everyone rummaging through cookbooks for ideas. I do hope this story will inspire you try one of the excellent commune pies that follow. And by the way, when I got to Colorado, I found that the peyote meeting had been canceled.

Mock Mince Pie

4 tart apples, cored and
  chopped
1/3 cup figs, snipped
1/3 cup dates, snipped
¼ cup sunflower seeds
¼ cup chopped walnuts
2 tablespoons sesame seeds

¼ cup honey
2 tablespoons molasses
1 teaspoon each cinnamon,
  allspice
½ teaspoon nutmeg
Crust for a single-crust pie

Combine all ingredients in a saucepan except the piecrust, and place over low heat. Bring to a boil; then simmer 15 minutes, stirring frequently. Meanwhile, heat oven to 400° and prebake the crust (see p. 24 for a suggestion on how to bake an empty pie shell) for 5 minutes. Pour in the filling, and bake 30 more minutes.

Marilyn, Vancouver Island

Carob Mint Cream Pie

1 tablespoon (1 package) gelatin
¾ cup milk
¼ cup honey
¼ cup carob powder, sifted
⅛ teaspoon salt
1 cup heavy cream

1 teaspoon finely crumbled
  dried mint or 1 tablespoon
  finely chopped fresh mint
Crust for a single-crust pie,
  baked (see note)

Sprinkle the gelatin on top of the milk, and let sit for a few minutes to soften. Then place in a saucepan or the top of a double boiler with the honey, carob powder and salt. Heat gently over boiling water or low heat, stirring, until the gelatin dissolves. Remove from heat, and chill until slightly thickened.

Whip the cream. Fold into the thickened carob mixture along with the mint. Turn into pie shell. Chill for an hour or two more, or until firm.

Note: For a suggestion on how to bake an empty pie shell, see p. 24. Or use Honey-Coconut Crust below.

Lorraine, Milkweed Hill, Vermont

Yogurt Pie

1 8-ounce package cream cheese
2 cups yogurt
2/3 cup honey
2 eggs
¾ teaspoon vanilla
¾ teaspoon almond extract
Crust for a single-crust pie, unbaked
2 tablespoons honey

Let the cream cheese soften at room temperature for an hour or two. Cream until smooth. Add 1 cup of the yogurt, 2/3 cup honey, the eggs and 1/2 teaspoon vanilla and almond extract. Beat well. Pour into an unbaked pie shell (see note) and bake at 350° for 40 minutes. Cool. Spread with topping: combine remaining yogurt, 2 tablespoons honey, and remaining vanilla and almond extract. Store pie refrigerated and covered to preserve the B vitamins in the topping.

Note: This pie is delicious baked in Honey-Coconut Crust, p. 196, which imparts a lovely coconut flavor. If you use it, however, bake in a straight-sided baking dish, or if you use a pie dish, cover only the bottom part of it with the crust, since any part that is exposed to prolonged heat will burn.

The Magic Bus, Oregon

Honey-Coconut Crust

1 cup untoasted wheat germ   ¼ cup oil
1/3 cup unsweetened coconut   2 tablespoons honey
¼ teaspoon salt

In a 9-inch pie pan, stir the dry ingredients together. (I've found that Pyrex pie plates are best for oven heating.) Mix in the oil and honey with a fork or your fingers, and stir well. Bake at 350° for 10 minutes. Watch carefully for overbrowning. Fill with any filling that doesn't require baking. It gets chewy, like candy. A true diehard vitamin freak, however, would chill rather than bake it, thus preserving the vitamin E in the wheat germ.

Terra Firma, Oregon

Fruit Pie Mistake

Roast dog was the least mouth-watering recipe offered to me anywhere (although Lou Gottlieb's Placenta Stew, a suggestion for the ritual disposal of the afterbirth, runs a close second). A dog had accidentally been killed at Peter Gray's Valley when it was caught stealing chickens, and the family decided it would be appropriate to eat it. They were so proud of themselves that the first recipe they mentioned was for "Bowserburgers." ("Tell them about *that* in your book," a friend of the commune urged me at the pie-baking contest. "Put a little yecccccccchhhhh in it so everyone won't rush in here and ruin the place.") The tamer vegetarians at the Moon Garden in Oregon sprouted mixed birdseed and made chapatis from it. A Jesus freak at Terra Firma told me to grind day-old sprouts and roll them out into thin chapatis, then put the cakes in the sun to "bake" all day, turning once at noon. This recipe, he said, came from the Essene Gospel of Peace. A kid I met in Eugene had roasted a deer in Polynesian fashion by burying it in the ground with hot rocks. At the Brush Brook Family in Oregon, one of the men had tried stir-frying carrot tops. "No, they weren't good," he reported. Marilyn of Vancouver Island, who likes to cram as much good stuff as she can into everything she makes, served me cookies containing almonds, peanuts, filberts, raisins, currants, sesame seeds, sunflower seeds, tahini, peanut butter, wheat germ, rye flakes, wheat flakes, oatmeal, eggs, vanilla, almond extract, spearmint leaves, honey, sea salt, seven grain flour, and carob powder. They were quite tasty, if hard to characterize. An artist I met at a backwoods community in California made me promise to mention his favorite snack: fried potatoes with grape jelly. The recipe below, however, is definitely the best of the weird ones. It was invented when David of High Ridge Farm mistook noninstant dry milk for flour while making a pie. The crust gets crisp on the bottom, custardy on top, and tastes delicious.

2½ cups noninstant dry milk	½ cup honey
½ teaspoon salt	1 teaspoon cinnamon
½ cup wheat germ	2 tablespoons lemon juice
1 cup oil	(optional)
4 to 5 tart apples, cored and	2 tablespoons butter
sliced	

Sift the dry milk and salt into a bowl. Add the wheat germ ("for a speckled effect," says David, a poet). With a fork, blend in the oil. (You may substitute water for

up to half of it, but your results will not be as crisp.)
Work into a pliable dough with fork or hands. Pat into
the bottom of an 8-by-8-inch baking pan or a pie pan.

Toss apples, honey, cinnamon, and, if the apples are
bland in flavor, lemon juice, in a bowl. Pour on top of
the crust and dot with butter. Bake in a preheated 350°
oven for 40 minutes.

Note: You may substitute any preferred fruit filling for
the apples.

Quick Apple Pie

They have a lot of ingredients for this pie at
Sunflower Farm in Ontario, where Jesse invented it,
because they run a nonprofit food co-op for local freaks
in their barn. Natural food staples are bought at
wholesale rates and sold without a markup in any
quantity. It's this sort of undertaking that transforms
the efforts of individual communes and homesteaders
into a movement.

6 tart unpeeled apples, sliced
2 tablespoons water
2 tablespoons honey (optional)
2 cups rolled oats
½ cup unsweetened coconut
¼ cup unsalted raw peanuts
¼ cup raw cashews, coarsely
chopped
¼ cup raisins
¼ cup currants (or an
additional ¼ cup raisins)
½ teaspoon salt
¼ pound sharp cheese,
sliced

Place apples and water in a heavy skillet or
saucepan. Cover, and cook over low heat until the
apples are soft, about 20 minutes. Sweeten with the
honey if you wish, or get into the natural, subdued
sweetness of the apples.

Preheat oven to 350°. Dry-roast the oats, coconut, nuts and fruit in a wok or skillet over medium heat, stirring, until the nuts are browned and the mixture gives off a good toasty smell. (See note.)

Pour the applesauce into an 8-by-8-inch pan. Top with the granola mixture, and spread the cheese on top. Bake for 10 minutes, or until the cheese is melted.

Note: Marjory adds that she browns the oatmeal mixture in 2 tablespoons oil, but this isn't necessary. Still, you might prefer it.

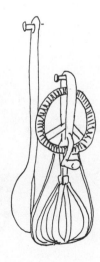

XII. Desserts and Candies

Baked Apples

In Lorraine's notebook of recipes at Milkweed Hill in Vermont (p. 32), I found this suggestion from a friend: "Core apples. Bake. Remove skins. Scrape goo off pan and inside of skins. Mix goo with wheat germ, sesame seeds, yogurt, cinnamon, cloves. Pour over apple insides. Arrange skins around dish like lettuce." Except until Mary figured it out, I thought she'd written "orange skins around dish like lettuce."

Banana Halvah

A farmer gave me a lift partway down the lonely
Oregon road to Evenstar, in the hills near the coast.
"You go down this road, and you come to a crick, and
then you come to another crick," he said when he let
me off. I asked how far it was. " 'Bout four miles," he
replied.

The road led through a verdant canyon. To one side
a river cascaded in a ravine. On the other, ferns clung
in profusion to the mossy rock wall. When my badly
balanced pack grew oppressive, I put my mouth to one
of the little springs that flowed from the rock and
drenched myself. On, on. It grew dark. I must have
tramped more like six miles without being passed by a
single car or finding the second "crick."

At last I came to a farmhouse with a collection of
junked cars at its gate. As I peered into the dark yard,
a man's voice hailed me from the shadows. "Is this
Evenstar?" I asked. "Yes," he answered. "The family's
out back. I was just milking the goat."

He led me behind the house to a circle around a
leaping campfire. "Welcome, sit down, rest, eat," soft
voices urged me. Someone handed me a coat-hanger
skewer with roasted vegetables and banana slices on
it. Gratefully, I ate and listened as the group described
its history. The family had come to Oregon together,
they said. A number of them had grown up together in
a Long Island suburb and first tried communal life in
the hills of northern New England. My roommate in
college had come from the same suburb. "Do you know
Winnie Frankel?" I asked.

"Winnie Frankel! Far out!" and so forth. Unexpectedly, I was home again.

Immediately these people drew me in with their open hospitality, their gentle fondness for one another. Although the commune included two children, they were discussing a suggestion that they try to adopt another as a family. When a joint was passed around, to make it go further each member exhaled the smoke into the mouth of the one next to him, as in some tribal rite of friendship. Most communes I visited were dominated by couples, who invariably slept in separate rooms or houses. Here everyone bedded in the attic of the farmhouse. There were several long-term pairs, but, I was told, they were becoming less intensely involved in their exclusive relationships. That night the attic reminded me of a small, friendly dormitory: several of the men played cards quietly by kerosene lamps while other members talked softly or read before falling asleep.

The next day we all lolled about naked in the sun and played at the family's favorite game. A swimming hole had been created in the river by a dam. Beside it, a shaky wooden tower about twelve feet high had been built and a thick piece of rope with a large knot in the end hung from a branch overhanging the pool. You climbed the tower, the rope was thrown up to you, you put the knot between your legs and jumped, the rope swinging back and forth until you dropped at last into the water. Everyone did it except me. Three times I climbed the tower, stared down nearsightedly, and gave up. "Do it!" shouts came up. "We were scared and we did it!" "Do it for the book!" But I couldn't do it, not even for the book. A girl visiting from a commune in southern California comforted me. "You don't have to do it," she said. "You'll still be loved if you don't." She was the only one who hadn't jumped yet either.

In the early evening, while some members prepared dinner, others worked at weaving belts, a source of communal income, on inkle looms. Again I was enchanted by Evenstar's special quality: a childlike closeness in every activity, a delight in sharing, giggling, cuddling. Another bond among them was a collective delight in sweets (p. 185). The following pudding, which you eat with a spoon, was adapted by David from a classical Indian recipe.

5 ripe bananas
¼ cup butter
2/3 cup water
½ cup honey

½ teaspoon rosewater or
    vanilla
½ teaspoon cardomon

Slice bananas into 1-inch rounds. Fry in butter several minutes over low heat, stirring. When lightly browned, remove from heat, and mash. Add water and honey. Simmer 15 to 20 minutes over low heat, or until thick. Remove from heat, and add flavorings. Pour into a serving dish, and serve warm or cold. Good with cream or yogurt. Serves 4 to 6. I gather that halvah is a generic term for sweets.

Yogurt Divinity Deluxe

2 cups yogurt
¼ cup sliced dates
1 orange, peeled and sliced

1 fig (ripe or dried), sliced
¼ cup honey
Unsweetened coconut

Combine all ingredients and sprinkle with coconut. Chill or eat at once. Store covered, to preserve B vitamins in yogurt.

Atlantis, Oregon

Honey Ice Cream I

I wish I had read Steve Diamond's exquisite book *What the Trees Said* (Delta Books, 1971) before I visited his commune in Massachusetts. I would have been so much more sensitive to the fabric woven by this close family, whose first members brought the Liberation News Service here from New York to find "a cultural . . . total and constant revolution" in their way of life, during four extraordinary years. As it was, I reacted mostly to the information that they, like their sister commune Total Loss Farm (p. 52), were planning to write up their own cookbook from the groovy things they ate. An old wooden crank freezer under the sink caught my eye, and I copied down the ice cream recipe which had been posted on a scrap of now-yellowed paper over the wood stove as long as anyone could remember, figuring it was in the public domain. Now that I've read Steve's book—a wonderfully detailed glimpse into commune life—I know where their ice cream really comes from: Dolly, the sloe-eyed cow, and her ponderous sister, Delilah, ravisher of gardens.

3 cups milk (see note)	Pinch salt
¾ cup honey	1 tablespoon vanilla
3 eggs, beaten	5 cups cream

Scald the milk (heat carefully just until a skin forms) in a double boiler over boiling water. Remove from heat, and stir in honey until it dissolves. Pour the milk mixture over the eggs, beating constantly. Return to double boiler, and heat, stirring frequently, until the mixture thickens. Remove from heat and add vanilla and salt. Chill.

When the custard is cold, add cream, and process in a churn freezer. Other flavoring ingredients, such as nuts (perhaps toasted or sautéed in butter) or crushed fruits, should be added during the churning, just when the ice cream has begun to thicken. Otherwise solids will sink to the bottom.

Our neighbor Albert, son of a backwoods dairy farmer whose people have been in the region for perhaps 150 years, churned our first batch of ice cream in the freezer we'd ordered from L. L. Bean. Ignoring the directions that came with it, he fitted the ice-cream container in the bucket and filled the latter with cracked ice (icicles put in a sack and smashed with a hammer) up to the top. He sprinkled about an inch of salt (no more, or the ice cream will freeze too fast) on the ice, then poured a kettle ("kittle," he calls it) of boiling water over the ice, saying, "You got to get the frost out of the ice." Then he put in another layer of ice and one of salt, keeping the water level just below the top of the container, which we had placed in a washtub to catch the melting ice. Albert cranked steadily for twenty minutes or so; cranking had always been his job when his large family made ice cream. When the mixture began to thicken, he opened the top of the container, and I added walnuts sautéed in butter. Albert was careful not to lift the container out of the bucket, pointing out that if he did, ice would get in underneath the container and prevent it from fitting in the bucket.

Our freezer has a fourteen-cup capacity, so I cut the recipe above by a third. When we poured the mixture into the freezer, it filled the container halfway; by the time we finished the ice cream had risen near the top, an expansion factor that must be reckoned with. Albert said we could eat the ice cream right away, but I would recommend removing the dasher, scraping the ice cream off it back into the container, then freezing the ice cream for several hours. We had ours with hot maple syrup on top. It was delicate and subtle.

Note: Ice cream need not be made with heavy cream; light cream or even half and half or top milk will do. Nor is the percentage of cream to milk hard and fast— you may alter it to suit.

Honey Ice Cream II

A sweeter and simpler version.

3 cups milk
3 cups cream
¾ cup honey

2 eggs, beaten
2 teaspoons vanilla
1 or 2 cups crushed fruit

Gently heat milk and cream, but try to remove from heat before a skin forms. Stir in honey, eggs and vanilla. Let cool, stirring until the honey melts. Process in a churn freezer as above. When it begins to thicken, add fruit; if the fruit is sour, increase honey in the ice cream mixture. Makes about 3 quarts.

The Mushroom Farm, California

Denise's Cheesecake

Denise lives in a communal house near New Paltz, New York. Her cooking is so famous in those parts that four unrelated people suggested I look her up. I asked all over town and finally found her in the local freak bar. You might call this lavish confection "Food Stamp Cheesecake," since that's about the only way a freak could afford to make it.

CRUST:

½ cup butter
1 ½ cups whole wheat pastry
   flour

½ teaspoon salt
1 tablespoon honey
1 egg, slightly beaten

Combine flour and salt. Work in the butter with your hands or a pastry cutter. When it is in tiny crumbs, add honey and the beaten egg. Pat the dough thinly over the bottom and sides of a 9-inch springform pan (essential for cheesecake and worth buying), up to a height of 2 inches. Chill for an hour, then bake at 350° for 10 minutes. (You may glaze the crust by brushing it before baking with one of the egg whites left from making the filling, blended with a little water.) Remove from the oven, then turn the heat up to 450°. Prepare the filling.

FILLING:

2 pounds cream cheese
½ cup honey (see note)
5 eggs
2 egg yolks
¼ teaspoon salt

3 tablespoons whole grain flour
   (Denise suggests corn flour)
1 teaspoon vanilla
½ teaspoon orange extract
½ teaspoon lemon extract

Have cream cheese at room temperature. Cream it with the honey and add the eggs and yolks one at a time, beating well after each addition. Blend in the salt and flour. Add the vanilla and fruit extracts, pour into the partially baked crust and bake at 450° for 10 minutes. Then lower heat to 275° and bake 1 hour more, or until a knife comes out clean. Then turn off the heat and leave in the oven 1 hour longer. If, like us, you use a wood stove, you can't do that fancy stuff; just bake at a moderate temperature until a knife comes out clean and remove from the oven, or put it in a hot oven and let the fire die down. Chill at least 8 hours before cutting.

Serve plain, or top with fruit such as strawberries or blueberries, with a couple of tablespoons of honey drizzled over them. For easy drizzling, heat the honey first.

Note: The original recipe called for 1 cup "raw" sugar rather than honey, and, instead of the extracts, the grated rind of 1 orange and 1 lemon. Since the "raw" sugar sold in this country is actually a form of processed sugar, it is not acceptable as a natural food. I changed the rinds to extracts because of the unknown shit that doubtless coats the fruit.

Sesame Halvah

1 cup sesame seeds	About ½ cup honey
½ cup instant or noninstant dry milk	1 teaspoon vanilla (optional)

Grind seeds in a grain mill. Combine with dry milk and enough honey to make a stiff dough. You may flavor the candy with vanilla. Roll into small balls. Makes about 30.

For coconut halvah, increase honey by 2 tablespoons and add 1/2 cup unsweetened coconut. For carob halvah, mix 2 tablespoons carob powder in with the sesame seeds. Other good additions are chopped nuts, raisins or currants, chopped dates or other dried fruit.

From suggestions by Gregory of the Brush
Brook Family in Oregon

High-Protein Candy Bars

Unforgettably good.

Condensed milk substitute:
1 2/3 cups instant dry
  milk or 1½ cups
  noninstant dry milk
2/3 cup fresh milk
1/3 cup honey
3 cups instant or noninstant
  dry milk
½ or ¾ cup fresh milk
  (see note)

½ cup oil
2 tablespoons vanilla
¼ teaspoon orange extract
  (optional)
1 heaping tablespoon aniseeds
½ cup raisins or currants
¼ cup chopped prunes
¼ cup chopped dried apricots
½ cup chopped or ground nuts
¼ cup chopped dates
½ cup unsweetened coconut

Condensed milk contains sugar, so first prepare this substitute. Put dry milk in a bowl. Gradually add fresh milk and honey. Blend until smooth.

To this, add the remaining ingredients gradually. Ground almonds are especially recommended as the nuts, since they "permeate the whole candy" with their flavor. Kathy Dutton of Happy Hollow, California, invented this originally for backpacking. Spread the sticky mixture in an oiled pan or on oiled aluminum foil and seal; it will harden up in a day, when you may cut it in squares. Or, roll into small balls and wrap well.

Kathy suggests you crack open the prune pits, chop the almond-flavored kernel inside, and add. These kernels, as well as raw almonds and the kernels in peach pits, are said to contain Vitamin B15, an alleged cancer preventative; but I take no stand on that.*

Other good additions include chopped dried figs and dried cherries (the latter something really delicious we recently discovered at Hatch's Natural Foods Store in

*For a discussion of Vitamin B15, see The Canadian Whole Earth Almanac's Healing issue (Vol. 2, No. 3), p. 154.

St. Johnsbury, Vermont), and well-drained unsweetened crushed pineapple.

Note: Use the smaller amount of fresh milk with instant
dry milk, the larger amount with noninstant dry milk.

The original recipe called for 2 heaping tablespoons
grated orange rind, which I can't countenance. Omit
the extract if you don't have any around; tastes
delicious without it.

Moonballs

Ron, strong, stern patriarch of twelve-or-so-member
Terra Firma in Oregon, came out of their farmhouse to
greet me. I explained my visit, and concluding, "I have
a present for you," pulled out a pound of cheese. Ron
shook his head. "We don't eat cheese here," he said,
"and besides, that kind's got preservatives in it." I
reddened as he explained that his family avoided
"mucus-forming" meat, dairy products and grains and
lived on uncooked fruits, vegetables, nuts and seeds as
much as possible. Later I went around to the other
members and tried to give away the damn cheese.
Finally, graciously, one woman accepted it. She stowed
it in a far corner of the refrigerator.

Ron's commitment to the organic way of life is
unusually strong, partly because he's determined to
bring up his young son uncontaminated by additives
and pesticides. Every week he drives a school bus to
Portland and loads it up with organically grown fruits
and vegetables, which he distributes to several food co-
ops in the Willamette Valley. Earning only enough
profit to pay for gas and oil, he works from the con-

viction that pure produce should be made available everywhere.

3 cups dates	1 cup wheat germ
1 cup raisins or currants	¼ cup rosehip power (see
1 cup almonds or other nuts	note) or ground fresh
1 cup sunflower seeds	rosehips
½ cup sesame seeds	Unsweetened coconut

Chop dates fine. Chop raisins, or use currants whole. Grind nuts and sunflower seeds in a grain mill, a blender or the fine blade of a meat grinder. Combine with sesame seeds, wheat germ and rosehip powder. If the dates are fresh and sticky, the mixture will hang together. Otherwise, add a little honey. Form into balls the size of marbles, and roll in coconut. Makes about 100.

Note: Some natural foods stores sell rosehip powder. It's been thoroughly exposed to the air, of course, which causes enzyme action that destroys vitamin C, so I doubt if any of the vitamin remains in it, but it will give the candy a nice tart bite. If you can't find the powder, you may grind up dried rosehips in a grain mill set for fine grind. Fresh rosehips, on the other hand, widely available in (unsprayed) gardens and by roadsides in the fall, are a super source of vitamin C.

Sesame Candy

3 cups sesame seeds
2 cups unsweetened coconut
1 cup chopped nuts
1 cup sunflower seeds
1½ cups honey

½ cup instant or noninstant
  dry milk
1 teaspoon vanilla
¼ teaspoon salt

Place the first four ingredients on an oiled baking sheet, and bake at 400° for 20 minutes, stirring occasionally.

Mix the honey and dry milk in a saucepan, and bring to a boil over medium heat, stirring. Remove from heat, and add vanilla and salt. Pour over the sesame mixture on the baking sheet. Let harden and cut into bars. A soft and chewy candy.

Terra Firma

XIII. Beverages

Communes often brew their own beer and wine or plan to start come spring. While it's technically illegal, nobody gets busted for brewing beer for home use. Before testing Crow Farm's* home brew method, I thought it would be a very valuable recipe. Crow is famous for its beer; up and down the West Coast I heard the Oregon commune referred to as a bunch of rowdy, beer-swilling chauvinist pigs who, among other apparently apocryphal stories, had brought TV dinners to the equinox party at Atlantis. I stopped in, rather fearfully, at a quiet time when most of the men were away on a job—Crow is also reputed to raise beef cattle for a living, but in fact they only keep a few for themselves—so I didn't get the full effect. The group I saw seemed drawn together both by family feelings and a shared love of comfort. Crow is one of the few

*More correctly, C.R.O. Farm, for Crow Research Organization.

communes I visited with a telephone and the only one with a pool table. In a room above the kitchen a floating population of adolescents, called teenybops, hung out, although I didn't look in to see what they did up there. The phone rang continually; once the girl who answered it shouted up the stairs, "Hey, teenybops! One of you come to the phone!" Meanwhile, James, who said he had once driven a cab in New York, served me a glass of the commune's excellent home brew. After testing Luke's recipe for it with disastrous results, I've learned more about beermaking, so I'm sure that next time I could succeed. If you are planning to brew for the first time, read the clear, simple directions below, consider my horrible failure with it, and finally, study my recommendations for improving the Crow method.

Luke's Home Brew

For a large batch of beer (which you shouldn't make unless you've collected enough bottles to put it all in), get a 20-gallon plastic garbage pail. (A crock or hogshead would be more desirable esthetically and ecologically.) Heat three 3-pound cans malt (see discussion that follows). Hop-flavored malt will give a tangy flavor and eliminate the need to add hops. Fill the pail two-thirds full of warm water and add 10 pounds sugar (see discussion that follows). Corn or invert sugar is said to be by far the best; it can be ordered through some winemaking supply houses,* and at Crow the supermarket orders it for them specially. Pour in the warm malt and sprinkle in a pinch of salt and 2 tablespoons yeast. (There's some

*See the list in *The Last Whole Earth Catalog,* p. 203.

controversy about what type of yeast to use; I've been told that baker's yeast will make a cloudy beer with a bready flavor, but others say that it does just as good a job as the more expensive brewer's yeast available at winemaking supply houses. At Crow they use plain baker's yeast.) If you are using unflavored malt and want an ale taste, add a handful of hops, boiled 15 minutes and strained into the brew. Stir up the brew with your arm until the sugar dissolves. Then put the container where you plan to leave it, someplace where it will stay warm. Add warm water up to 3 inches from the top. Cover and let sit for a theoretical 5 to 7 days. In this time, the primary fermentation period, the beer will "work," as the yeast converts the sugar to alcohol and causes carbon dioxide to be released. When carbon dioxide bubbles stop coming to the surface and the brew no longer tastes sweet, or when a brew tester, a gadget available at winemaking supply houses, indicates that all the sugar has been converted into alcohol, the brew is ready to bottle. Some experienced brewers bottle just before the brew stops working, so the last CO_2 released is trapped to carbonate the bottled beer, but the Crow system is to wait until the beer is completely flat and put 1/4 teaspoon sugar in the bottom of each 12-ounce bottle or a rounded 1/4 teaspoon in each quart bottle. This sugar will ferment (the secondary fermentation period), and the bubbles will be trapped in the bottle. Too much sugar, however, will cause explosions (see below).

Siphon the brew into the sterilized bottles. Cap with a bottle capper, or use twist-top beer or wine bottles. Check the latter to make sure the top is on tightly; if not, dip the top into melted paraffin to seal. Store the bottles in a dark place for 30 days or more to get really

good, although you can start drinking after 5 days. The
yeast will settle to the bottom, so keep the bottles
upright and don't joggle them. To serve, chill the beer,
then pour it carefully into a pitcher or glasses, without
disturbing the sediment. You can save the sediment to
use as nutritional yeast.

So went the recipe Luke gave me. I mixed up half a
batch in a 10-gallon plastic garbage pail around
Thanksgiving and set it behind the wood stove. Three
weeks later, presumably because it got chilled every
night when the stove went out, the brew was still
bubbling faintly, but since I was about to leave for two
weeks in New York, I ladled it into gallon jugs with a
cautious 1-1/2 teaspoons sugar in each. When I came
back from the city, I found that the bottles had frozen
solid. Righteously pissed, I put them all up in the loft
above the wood stove, the only place in the house that
stays more or less warm all the time. While they sat, I
began getting advice from any number of beermakers.
One visitor told me that you should have at least 1
pound sugar per gallon water, or the beer will be
weak—a proportion which the books I've consulted
confirm. Another said that the reason you have to
siphon, not ladle, the beer out is to avoid getting the
yeasty sediment, or "mother," into the bottles. He also
pointed out that my recipe called for 50 percent too
much malt extract, an excess which would make the
beer heavy and bitter.

Then one evening in early January I was sitting by
the wood stove reading while the rest of the family was
upstairs in the loft getting ready for bed. Suddenly we
heard a dull boom, followed by a cascade of foam down
the wall. Upstairs, they thought at first that a kerosene
lamp had exploded, but I knew what had happened by

the foam: "A beer bottle exploded!" "If one goes, they'll all go," Robert shouted, horrified, and we rushed to loosen the caps. The third cap wouldn't budge. I tried it, Mary tried it, then we stepped back to let Robert try. He was just reaching forward when the bottle blew up, sending brew and glass everywhere. Robert gropingly loosened the rest with one of us holding a towel over his eyes. Later we found a piece of glass lodged in the beam above the bottles by the force of the explosion.

My errors were obvious: I bottled the beer too soon and allowed the "mother" to contaminate the bottles. Apparently the recipe also was at fault, because my beer was low on alcohol and very malty. The Crow method is convenient and simple, but I would double the sugar and reduce the malt to 2 cans for a 20-gallon batch or 1 can for a 10-gallon batch. I would try to keep the beer at a fairly steady heat between 60° and 70° during the primary fermentation period, and in particular I would not bottle the brew until no more than two or three bubbles a minute rose to surface when I disturbed it. I've found a siphon: a length of plastic tubing used for collecting maple sap. A hollow plastic jump rope, cut open, works well but more slowly.

Further remarks: At a communal house in Eugene I met Richard, another dedicated brewer. He pointed out that if you use water from a city system, the chlorine will kill the yeast, so substitute distilled water for it, or let the water stand for a couple of days, so the chlorine will evaporate. He also recommends using marijuana instead of hops. They're in the same family, and grass will give the beer a good flavor.

For a helpful discussion of beermaking see *Mother Earth News, No. 4,* pp. 68-69.

Judy's Honey Wine

I turned up this intriguing recipe at Atlantis in Oregon, in a pile of recipes written out in various hands. A month later, I spent the afternoon at Plate Rock Ranch in California (p. 141). While I sat in the kitchen talking to Leslie, a lady named Judy, who was staying at a commune nearby, dropped in. She was excited when she heard that I'd visited Atlantis, since she'd spent some time there. I told her all the news. Later she said, "I should give you my recipe for honey wine." "Gee, I already have a recipe for honey wine," I replied. "I found it at Atlantis, as a matter of fact. Judy's Honey Wine." Then the light dawned.

I have altered the proportions to increase the alcohol content of this light wine.

3 ounces fresh gingerroot or	a hammer
1½ ounces dried gingerroot	5 pounds honey
2½ tablespoons whole cloves	3 gallons water
2½ tablespoons nutmeg or 4	1 package wine yeast
nutmegs, crushed with	

Slice the fresh gingerroot, or grind dried gingerroot in a grain mill set on coarse grind. Put cloves, nutmeg and ground ginger in a clean sock, and knot it; if you use fresh gingerroot, put it directly in the wine mixture.

In a large kettle, bring the honey and 1 gallon of the water to a boil. Boil 5 minutes over medium heat. Add the sock and gingerroot, and boil 5 more minutes.

Pour the honey mixture, sock and ginger into a crock or plastic garbage pail, and add 2 more gallons of water. Stir well; then sprinkle in yeast. Keep the container in a warm place, covered. After two weeks, remove the sock and ginger. Let the brew sit undisturbed until fermentation is finished and bubbles no

longer rise to the surface when you disturb it, which
may take several more weeks. Siphon into sterilized
bottles. You may start drinking the wine right away,
but it gets better as it matures. However, meads (honey
wines) should be drunk within a year.

Note: The original recipe called for 2-1/2 tablespoons
cassia buds, whatever they are; include them by all
means if you can find them.

Buoy Bill's Rice and Raisin Wine

Country freaks are more likely to celebrate the
solstices and equinoxes than most traditional holidays.
For the summer solstice, the longhairs who have
thickly settled the Salwaka Valley in Oregon actually
formed an entertainment committee, collected money,
and threw a party down by the community garden, a
plot open to anyone to cultivate and harvest. That June
afternoon, placid family groups gathered in an oak
grove nearby. While the children romped, the so-called
adults talked quietly and made conversational music
on guitars, drums, mandolins and flutes. Tubs of beans
and salad had been contributed; Elaine of High Ridge
Farm brought her favorite multipurpose salad, rice
with an oil and vinegar dressing and any crunchy
vegetables and pickles she felt like adding. To the
delight of some and disgust of others, the entertainment committee provided cartons of cheap hot
dogs, which were roasted on sticks over a bonfire.
Buoy Bill and I met while we were leaning against the
same tree. He gave me this recipe, his only one. When I
asked him how good it was, the rough woodsman in-
dignantly answered, "Would I carry a five-gallon crock
wherever I go if it wasn't good?"

After dinner, a power line was run in and Duck Soup, a California band, set up its equipment. They swung into a set of lively good-time tunes with a delightful beat. Then free LSD was passed around. Swept by indescribably powerful waves of group energy, the crowd danced passionately for hours. I ascended into another, more wonderful level of consciousness, and consequently left my shoulder bag behind when the folks from High Ridge Farm took me home. An hour before dawn I walked the mile back to the community garden to look for it, under stars that still danced a little. The band had packed up and gone, but the fire leaped on, and around it the last revelers still swayed to the atonal blowing of flutes. It was the first morning of summer.

This wine is no LSD, but it's good enough for Buoy Bill.

4 cups rice	5 gallons warm water
2 pounds raisins	1 package wine yeast
12 pounds sugar	

In a 10-gallon plastic garbage pail or crock place rice, raisins and sugar. Add the water and stir until the sugar dissolves. Sprinkle in the yeast. Cover loosely, but keep a stick in the container, and stir the mixture whenever you walk by for 3 days. Then let sit undisturbed for 5 to 8 weeks, or until fermentation has stopped. Don't let it sit too long, or it will turn to vinegar. Use 15 pounds of sugar for a stronger drink. Siphon off and bottle. Let stand for several months in a dark, cool place before drinking.

Note: There is an excellent discussion of winemaking in *The Last Whole Earth Catalog*, pp. 202-3.

Sima, "a Bubbly Mead"

This is quickly made and tastes like a light car-
bonated lemonade. But I don't know how to circumvent
my scruples about lemon peels. Do you? See if you can
find organic lemons.

2 lemons	⅛ teaspoon baker's yeast
1 cup honey	Raisins
1 gallon water, boiling	

Peel the lemons. Slice them finely, and place the
peels and honey in a container. Pour on boiling water.
Let cool until lukewarm; then stir in yeast. Let sit
loosely covered for 12 hours; then bottle, adding 3
raisins per bottle. When the raisins have floated to the
top, in a day or two, chill and serve.

Rainbow City Hall, Vancouver

I made this all in one container. I cut the lemons
small and put them and the peels in a gallon bottle.
Then I dissolved the honey in the water and poured
them through a funnel. After letting the mixture sit for
12 hours, I dropped in 3 raisins and tightened the cap.
We drank it with dinner the next day.

Yoga Tea

I certainly hadn't planned to go from San Francisco
to Taos by way of Cheyenne, Wyoming. When I went
over to University Avenue in Berkeley with a "New
Mexico" destination sign, I was counting on getting a
ride south toward Arizona, from where it was an easy

drive of two days to Taos. After two hours of fruitless
waiting, a young man pulled into the gas station behind
me. Ignoring the five boys on my block alone with signs
that read *East*, he sidled up to me, murmuring, "I'll
take you to Sacramento"—a short ride away on Interstate 80, which runs east across Nevada, Utah and
Wyoming. "Damn," I thought, but I was tired of
waiting, so, resigning myself to the weary haul across
the deserts and the mountains, I accepted.

We pulled onto the freeway. I was just rolling a joint
from the driver's stash when we saw a car ahead of us
with Arizona plates. Hope revived. I wrote "Going to
Arizona?" in my notebook and held it up for the young
couple inside. The girl in the passenger seat rolled
down her window to yell, "No, Tahoe!" Hope died
again; the lake lay due east, on the Nevada border. "I'll
go!" I shouted back. They pulled over, and I changed
cars. And it turned out to have been in the Flow after
all. The girl gave me this recipe, from an ashram near
Tucson.

1 teaspoon whole cloves	10 cardomon seeds
¼ teaspoon black peppercorns	1 quart water
2 sticks cinnamon	
2 1-inch pieces dried gingerroot	

Cover the spices with the water, bring to a boil,
reduce heat, and simmer 45 minutes. Strain and serve.
At the ashram, the lady said, this was served with a
mixture of honey, goat's milk and almond oil. This oil is
available in pharmacies and natural foods
stores. A friend returned from the Himalayas told me

that it is commonly used there and is pressed from the kernels inside peach or plum pits. (See p. 193 for mention of the possible properties of these kernels. Once you taste you'll crack your pits forever.)

The tea grows stronger on standing, so if you leave the spices in the unused part, you may have to dilute it later.

XIV. Condiments, Preserves and Snacks

Soy Spread

This glorious, original spread from the Motherlode in Oregon can be served by itself as a sandwich spread or used as a vegetable substitute for mayonnaise.

1 cup soy flour
2½ cups water
2½ cups oil
Juice of 1 lemon
4 to 5 cloves garlic, mashed

1 tablespoon honey
2 tablespoons tamari
½ teaspoon curry powder
½ teaspoon paprika
¼ teaspoon salt

Combine soy flour and water in a heavy saucepan. Bring to a boil over medium heat, stirring frequently. Then lower heat, and simmer 20 minutes, stirring occasionally. Cool. Add remaining ingredients. Makes 1 quart.

Chutney

2½ cups chopped dates
2 cups chopped prunes
4 tart apples, cored and
    chopped
1 beet, peeled and chopped
1 cup raisins
1 onion, chopped
2 cloves garlic, mashed
1/3 cup honey

2/3 cup molasses (see note)
¾ cup cider vinegar
1 teaspoon nutmeg
½ teaspoon black pepper
1 teaspoon cloves
1½ teaspoons cinnamon
½ teaspoon ginger
1½ cups water

Combine all ingredients in a large, heavy pot. Bring to a boil over medium-low heat, stirring frequently. Reduce heat, cover, and simmer 1 hour. Add more water if it becomes too dry. You may pour into sterilized 4-pint or 2-quart jars and seal. Or if you don't want to bother, you can just store it in jars; kept cool, the vinegar and sugar will prevent it from spoiling. Serve with curries.

Note: If you use blackstrap molasses, reduce to 1/3 cup and increase honey to 2/3 cup.

Bibs Family, Vermont

Highbush Cranberry Ketchup

Highbush cranberries ripen in northern states in the fall. The fire-engine red berries are even better after a frost. This recipe is adapted from a University of Alaska pamphlet on Alaskan flora which found its way by some means to the Magic Bus in Eugene, Oregon. It yields a puree that looks and tastes like an exotic tomato ketchup.

12 cups highbush cranberries
3 onions, finely chopped
2 cups cider vinegar
2 cups honey
1 teaspoon salt

1 tablespoon cloves
1 tablespoon cinnamon
1 tablespoon allspice
1 tablespoon celery seed
1 teaspoon black pepper

Combine all ingredients in a large kettle. Bring to a boil, reduce heat, and simmer 2 hours. Grind in a meat grinder, food mill, grain mill or blender, and strain out the seeds. Pour into sterilized jars and seal. Makes 3 pints.

We were sitting around the campfire my first night at Peter Gray's Valley in New Mexico, roasting hot dogs on sticks and experimenting with a new invention that involved a banana, a chocolate bar, a graham cracker and a toasted marshmallow. Mary Jo remarked that since snacking outrageously is as much a part of commune life as dining righteously, why didn't I put all my zuzu* recipes in one chapter and call it "Geezes and Scarfs"? I don't know what a geeze is, but to scarf is to eat, with the connotation of greed. Communards do scarf, but not always on junk food (geezes?). Following are a few commune mid-meals, light lunches and snacks that need no apology.

Soy Nuts

I was in a natural foods store in Vancouver when a middle-aged lady came up to the girl in charge and thanked her for explaining how to roast soy beans. She had been experimenting with the method all week and

*High-carbohydrate junk food.

had finally perfected it. I asked her how she did them now, and she told me, saying that she had baked batches at all different temperatures and laid them out. Her family agreed that the best ones were those roasted at 425°.

Cover soy beans with water. Remove those that float to the surface. Soak overnight. The nutrients will be best preserved if the beans absorb as much of the soaking water as possible. Drain them the next day, and toss in a bowl with enough oil to coat and some salt. Spread on a baking sheet. Bake at 425° for 15 to 20 minutes, stirring often.

Note: Debbie of Prairie Dog Village in California says that the soybeans will be crisper if you drain them on a towel or paper towel and dry them (uncovered, or they'll sprout) for three days. She also recommends sprinkling them lightly with garlic powder after roasting.

Nachos

Quarter Corn Tortillas (p. 92). Heat 2 tablespoons oil in a skillet over high heat, and brown the tortilla quarters until crisp—a minute or two. Salt lightly. Put on a baking sheet in a single layer. Cut slices of sharp cheese slightly smaller than the tortilla pieces, and place one slice on each. Slice jalapeño peppers or small green chilies, skinned (p. 23) and seeded or not, depending on your taste for heat, 1/4 inch thick, and lay a slice on top of the cheese. Bake in a hot oven until the cheese melts—a few minutes. Eat as a snack or as an accompaniment to soup or salad.

The Furry Freak Brothers, New Mexico

Empanaditas

Lucille of the Furry Freak Brothers is of Mexican ancestry. This is one of her grandmother's recipes. Its mixture of fruits, sweetener and meat reminds one of mincemeat. I'm not sure whether I'd serve these with dinner or for dessert, so I copped out and put them here.

2 tart apples, cored and diced	or chicken
1 tablespoon honey	1 teaspoon cinnamon
1 carrot, grated	½ teaspoon nutmeg
1 / 3 cup raisins, currants,	¼ teaspoon salt
chopped dates or prunes	Pastry for a single-crust pie
½ cup shredded boiled beef	

Place the apples in a saucepan with the honey, and toss to coat. Cover and place over low heat. Simmer for 15 minutes. Remove from heat, and add remaining ingredients except pastry.

Divide the pastry into 8 or 16 equal parts. Roll each one out thinly on a floured board. Place a good spoonful of the filling mixture in each circle, fold over, and press around the edges with a fork to seal.

Preheat oven to 400°. Heat 1/8 inch oil in a skillet. Fry the turnovers briefly over medium-high heat to brown; then place on a baking sheet. Bake empanaditas 20 minutes. Makes 8 large or 16 small empanaditas.

Breakfast Tacos

Tortillas form the basis of many breakfasts and lunches in New Mexico. At the Lama Foundation, near Taos, a favorite breakfast consists of a corn tortilla heated on a griddle, covered with grated sharp cheese, avocado slices and sprouts, seasoned with tamari and folded. (My Vermont Corn Tortillas, p. 92, become too crisp to fold when baked on a griddle, but take better to frying in a little oil.) Also for breakfast, Lisa, elsewhere in New Mexico (p. 74), sautéed corn tortillas in butter until lightly browned, folded them and filled them with cream cheese, sprouts and tamari. She would also have added chopped watercress and avocado if she had them.

Potatoes and Rice

Late in the evening at Holy Earth in California, two of the men arrived home from an all-day job to find supper eaten. One of them chopped a couple of onions and sautéed them in oil until brown with leftover brown rice, 2 or 3 mashed cloves of garlic and a cubed potato. Then he covered the skillet until the potato was tender. Good served with tamari and a fried egg.

Eggs with Banana and Yogurt

Fred, a scholarly-looking fellow at High Ridge Farm in Oregon, ambled into the kitchen one evening and scrambled some eggs with yogurt and a sliced banana. Just 2 eggs and 1/4 cup yogurt beaten together with 1 banana sliced in thinly, poured into a small heated skillet with a little oil or butter in it, set over low heat until the mixture begins to thicken, then scrambled with a fork, makes enough for one. Singularly good.

Index

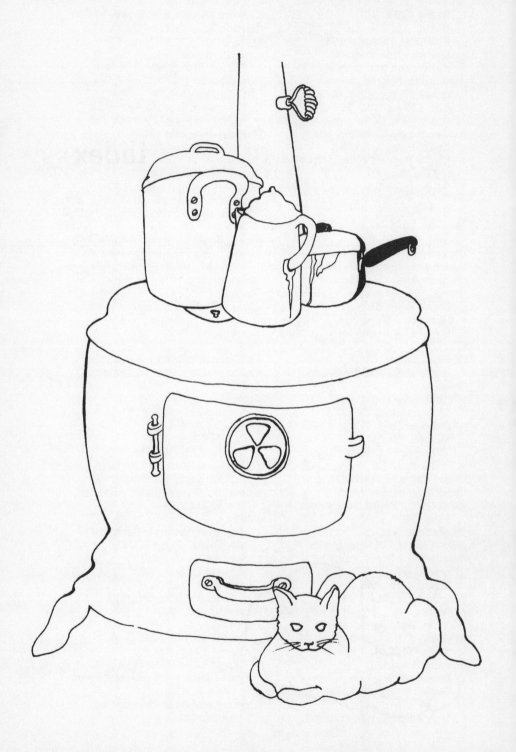